GLOW TO GOLD

Created by:

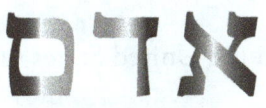

Adam

Copyright © 2024 Adam
All rights reserved
First Edition

NEWMAN SPRINGS PUBLISHING
320 Broad Street
Red Bank, NJ 07701

First originally published by Newman Springs Publishing 2024

ISBN 979-8-89308-570-9 (Paperback)
ISBN 979-8-89308-571-6 (Digital)

Printed in the United States of America

On a midsummers BREEZE
                A Glowie came out
                              To take a PEAK

        What he saw with his eyes
        Nothing could COMPARE

      It was the most beautifulest golden girl
      With the most gorgeous of HAIR

          As he walked closer
          Eyes starring in a GAZE

        He got a burn on his arm
           Ran into a pole
      Then heard somebody shout out
              His NAME

BRIGHT: Hey, FREAK!
              What are you doing down there?

      LIGHT: Did you hit your head or something?

BRIGHT: Ha-ha, yeah, DUFUS!

           With his head down,
        Embarrassed and ASHAMED.

He heard a soft voice that would soon change his heart

                          That very DAY.

SHINE: It's okay to fall sometimes. It's how you RISE up that matters. Here, let me help you.

        As she reached out her hand

Glow to Gold

And started to get CLOSE,
Her fingers turned black as sackcloth,
And he glowed like a GHOST.

Shine: Ahh, ahhh! You're a Glowie? You're not supposed to be here.

Bright: OMG SHINE, let's go.

With hope in her eyes
And with a sad SMILE,

She waves him goodbye
And says
Shine: Maybe I'll see you TOMORROW.

As he looked up
With a tear welling in his EYE,

He says with a whisper:

Aldin: Her name is SHINE.

With a grin on his FACE,

He skips to his PLACE,

Into the darkest of the wilderness
Where he likes to
ESCAPE.

I met this girl
Fit for a golden KING.

So what would she ever want
With a poor little Glowie like ME?

Adam

I hide in the shadows
She dances in the LIGHT.

Her heart is full of joy
And mine is dark as NIGHT.

She's happy

I'm SAD

She's good

I'm BAD

We're Yin and YANG
She's amazing and I'm
LAME
For us to be united is an Abomination and SHAME
But there has to be a way
I hope someone can pull some STRINGS

I've never felt this way before
Just her smile makes my heart SING

I have to see her again
I have to seek this THROUGH

I think what I'm feeling right now is love
This must be the TRUTH

Nothing is what it SEEMS
A Glowie's night is full of MEAN

But for me to be feeling what I'm feeling
This can't be just a
DREAM

WyUlle: Aldin!
What are you doing? You're late. Dad's been looking for you.

Glow to Gold

ALDIN: Yes, yes, yes, I know. I'm on my way now.

        Through the thick dead TREES
           Into a world UNSEEN

        There's a neon-colored KINGDOM
        That has taken away all FREEDOM

With a shrug of his shoulders
                              And with a soft SIGH
Aldin mumbles to himself
   ALDIN: There goes my dominion and the rest of my LIFE.

           On his way DOWN
       Looking at all the Glowie's FROWN

They stop with their work
                      And gather in front of Tazan
           The leader of the TOWN
             With a fake smile
          Aldin waves and NODS

       Tazan rushes him center stage
            And says
TAZAN: Now that was the last
              TIME!

TAZAN: HEAR-HE, HEAR-HE! My fellow Glowies from the Gloomy Night, tonight is a night of celebration. A roar for an UPRISING!

GLOWIES: Yay! (*Applause and cheers*)

    TAZAN: Now I know we don't glow like we used to, but with Aldin, the new Head of Spray, we will glow brighter than ever before!

4   *Adam*

GLOWIES: Yay! (*Applause and cheers*)

TAZAN: Aldin, step forward! With my son Aldin, the new Head of Spray. He shall be doused with our new brew, and glow our new glow, for our new age!

GLOWIES: Yay! (*Applause and cheers*)

With one little squeeze
Aldin's covered in SPRAY

His flames grew bigger and brighter
                                                            With an explosion of light
In a very gloomy WAY

With his flame burning brighter
Shocked and DAZED

The crowd was all stunned
                                                       In the Gloomiest of WAYS

TAZAN: Ha-ha-ha, back to work my Glowies! Let's work, let's build, let's create! Now work, work, work. Ha-ha-ha!
Come, Aldin.
This is a huge responsibility, which should not be taken lightly. The fate of our world lies in your hands now. It's time to grow UP and be the prince you were born to be! After tonight, your new life starts. So take the rest of the night, go to the mushroom field, and spray it with our new brew. Get one with the spray and embrace what you are destined for!

Aldin: But what if this isn't me? What if I can't do what you want? I'm sure WyUlle would be better at all of this than me.

Tazan: FOOL! Don't you dare speak to me in that way!
Your brother is nothing but a voice! You are my prized
possession! You are my image, and my will shall be done!
Now get back to work, and I don't want to hear
another fantasy of yours. This is your life now,
get used to it. Now out of my sight!

With Aldin's dad forcing this new LIFE
                        He slowly walks to the mushroom field
Feeling grumpy and SPITE

                        Kicking over mushrooms
And angrily spraying the SITE

                        He spots something golden
It's a little scroll of LIGHT

Aldin: Whoa, what is that?

Digging it up from the ground
He opens the golden SCROLL
A vision over takes him
Transforming him to GOLD

THE VISION

He sees a WHITE DOG
And his dad, Tazan
As a golden MAN

He watches him get mad
As he falls to the LAND

Tazan turns into a SNAIL

Glowing and SCALED

He yells to the clouds
As his followers FELL

Angry with everything
Tazan conquers the land with FEAR

Hiding in the shadows and keeping the golden ones NEAR

Stealing their light from the day
To make their night GLOW

Aldin gets a realization
Of just who Tazan is and how this truth needs to be
TOLD

Coming back TO

And looking very CONFUSED

Aldin speaks out loud

Aldin: Holly molly! What did I just see? This so can't be TRUE!

Walking back and forth in a PACE
His heart in a RACE

He notices that he's turned golden
And panics to hide his FACE

Aldin: Ahh, ahhh! Oh my gosh, oh my gosh, oh my gosh! Oh no! Oh no! Oh no!

He rushes and hides
Behind the biggest mushroom in the FIELD

He takes a deep breath
Knowing the truth was REVEALED

Aldin: Okay, okay Aldin, get it together. Woe, I'm Golden! How, how am I still in the dark?.

Greeby: HEY, ALDIN! Where are you? It's your best pals, Greeby and Sfary!

Sfary: Hello, Aldin! Don't be holding out on us. We want to try that new spray! You can't just keep it all to yourself.

Greeby: Yeah! Ha-he-he! You owe US for putting up with your brother!

ALDIN: I can't let them see me like this.
I have to get out of here.

GREEBY: Yo, Aldin! Quit being a little punk and get out here!

SFARY: Yeah, give us that spray! We deserve it!

With Aldin in a rush
                                    To escape the Gloomy NIGHT

He left behind the spray
                Something he should have
                Never
                FORGOT

Heart so BOLD
                                          And out of CONTROL

                First time in his life
          He's filled with happiness and JOY

With such strong focus and only one thing on his MIND

       Aldin's off to find the most precious of gold
                A girl named
                SHINE

          But back in the Gloomy Night
          Deep into the mushroom FIELD

            An event will take place
         That will have Aldin's fate SEALED

SFARY: Greeby Look! I found the spray.

GREEBY: He-he-he! Very good, Sfary. Aldin, we got your spray! Come out. Come out, wherever you are!

SFARY: Forget him. Come on spray me. Spray me.

GREEBY: Okay. Hold still.

Spray.

Oh MY, Sfary! Look at those eyes and that smile. Very scary. How does it feel?

SFARY: This feels awesome! Check out this glow! Grrr! Ha-ha! Come on. Your turn. Let me see it!

Spray.

Dang, Greeby! LOOK at you! You're claws and those fangs you have. That's so creepy!

GREEBY: Ohh! This feels good. He, he! This is more than just a new glow. This is, this is…

TAZAN: What are you TWO doing?

GREEBY: Uhh…
SFARY: We were just… Uhh…

TAZAN: Give me that, and get out of my SIGHT!
Tazan staring down at the hole
Having such evil in his EYE

That great hate in his heart
Started to ARISE

Laughing with frustration and anger
                                              He gives out a deep SIGH

Tazan starts to speak into existence
The most horrible of LIES
Tazan: Oh, Aldin, my son.
What have you done?
The Golden Day will be mine!
And if I have to take you down with it, so be IT.
You better be ready to choose. The takeover starts now.

Now Aldin's at the threshold of crossing over
To the golden DAY

Not sure how to act
                        Nerves and fear came to PLAY

Heart beating fast
He takes a deep BREATH

                    Hopping right into the golden Day
                    He says…

ALDIN: Whew, okay. I can now RELAX.

As the bus passes by
Aldin sees Shine INSIDE

With the biggest grin on his face
              He waves
            Running BEHIND

Shine notices this unfamiliar boy waving crazy to her
Through the WINDOW

Then her friends Bright and Light started
busting out with laughter
Saying…

BRIGHT: OMG, Shine, check out this **WEIRDO**!

With a giggle and a smile
                   Shine gently waves
                   BACK

         Aldin tries to run faster
         Then trips from a CRACK

          Everyone is laughing
Aldin walks off into some bushes to HIDE

A memory came to Shine
                   About the Glowie that CRIED
          Getting off the bus
         She looks to the Great TREE

         Filled up with hope inside
         But there was no Glowie to SEE

           Sitting in the bushes
         Feeling so silly and STUPID

         This little white dog finds Aldin
              Barking
           Wearing a collar
       With the name written Q-Pit

ALDIN: Hey there, little guy. What are you doing? Huh, you barking at me?
Q-Pit.
That's a cute name for a cute little doggy.

Q-PIT: Bark! Bark! Bark!

ALDIN: What, What is it boy?

Adam

Q-Pit: Bark! Bark! Bark!

ALDIN: I can't understand you. What are you trying to say?

Q-Pit: Bark! Uhuhuhuhuhu.

ALDIN: Umm, okay, you want me follow
you to that big empty castle?

Q-Pit: Bark! Bark! Huhuhuhuhuhuhu.

ALDIN: Okay, following you.

                 Walking toward what seemed to be
An abandon
      Golden
            CASTLE

                 Aldin spots a statue of a white dog
                    And it's holding out a
                           SATCHEL

                       As he gets closer
           He sees his name "Aldin" written on IT

                   Curious as he is now
          He takes it into his hands and WONDERS

                Opening up the satchel
           He hears this voice come OUT

*Aziz: Aldin, Aldin, listen!
I have chosen you for a purpose.
The fallen Tazan is preparing to make war upon the Golden Ones.
He believes he has stolen enough light from the Golden
Day, to empower his fearful Glowie army. You are the
only one that knows what a Glowie's weakness is.
All you have to do is know it in your heart.
That light will always outshine dark!
If you can understand this without doubt, then everything
else you seem to need will fall right into place.*

Just believe, Aldin. Believe!

ALDIN: Woah! What in the GLOOM was that?
           What is happening to me?

Q-PIT: Bark, bark, huhuhuhuhuhu, bark.

ALDIN: No, wait! Where are you going? Wait for me!
           You're the only one I know here.

Being all ALONE
And feeling like he's shunned from his HOME.

Aldin walks in amazement through the golden castle,
Seeing ancient pictures of the Golden Day
He starts to ROAM.

Going from room to room
                    And down a sacred HALL,

He puts the art around him together
And discovers exactly
What began it
ALL.

ALDIN: So Aziz is the White Dog, and my dad was his first creation?
    His name used to be Gright, Bringer of the Great Light.
        His pride in wanting to become like Aziz
        caused him to fall and turn into Tazan.
     The Gloomy Night was only created because
        Tazan wasn't allowed into the Golden Day.
    So that means we were all supposed to be Golden!
    I still don't know what a Glowie's weakness is, though.
        Is it that we're mean and careless? Ha-ha, no.
        Could it be that we're all differently unique,
             with strange Glowie abilities?
Nah, definitely not. What about all we know how to do is work?

Glow to Gold   15

BOOM!
Hey, what's that?

After hearing something hit the GROUND
Aldin goes searching and looking AROUND.

The sound he found to HEAR
Makes him quiet and tiptoe NEAR,

Sneaking closer and closer
With his back against the WALL.

Unsure of what it is
But he knows it's the most wonderfulest
Sound of ALL.

Shine: Uhmm, uhmm
Umhmm, uhmm
Oh Glowie, my GLOWIE
Where were you today, my mysterious GLOWIE?
I was hoping to see YOU.
I was hoping to meet YOU.
I felt a connection while touching your hand
That I hope is not MISLEADING.

I know this is FORBIDDEN
like the fruit that was EATEN
But why, oh why do I have this FEELING
That if you're not in my life
The air that I breathe will turn to
FREEZING
There must be a reason
I mean, I know I don't even know you,
And you have my heart BEATING.
The green in your eyes
Has the gold of me GLEAMING.

Adam

Oh, how I wish you were here.
Oh, I WISH
I WISH, I WISH.
I just can't stop thinking of you.
Oh, how I long for your…

Aldin: Hello! I do believe your wish has come true.

Shine: Ahh, ahhh, ahhh!
Who are you? What do you want?
How did you find me?
This is my place of comfort!
Are you a creep?

Aldin: Oh my gosh, that was so dumb of me.
Stupid Aldin, stupid, stupid, stupid!
I am so sorry; I didn't mean to bother you.
Your singing was beautiful; I had to see who it was.

Shine: You were stalking me? What's wrong with you?
You are a creep. Get out!

Aldin: No, no, I wasn't stalking you!
I was just wandering around this castle
and heard someone else here.

Shine: So what! You think that gives you
the right to barge in here on me?
Do you not have any respect?

Aldin: Okay, yes, you're right. That was very
wrong of me. Let me start over.
Hi, I'm Aldin.

Shine: Well hello there, AL…donn!
That's a strange name. And I am…

Glow to Gold

SHINE AND ALDIN: Shine.

As a lock of their eyes
        And a stare so deep it created
                            PASSION.

        They will not know it yet
        But true love's magic
        Had just
        HAPPENED.

        Lost in the moment
Both their worlds were FORGOTTEN.

Everything around them faded away
        And it seemed like life's confusion
                Was SOFTENED.

Forgetting how to speak
Only seeing the existence of them TWO.

        Shine finally speaks out some words
                And says…

SHINE: I feel like I know YOU.
        Aldin, not sure how to explain
        He plunders in THOUGHT.
        He says…

    ALDIN: We met yesterday under the Great Tree;
        I'm that Glowie your heart CAUGHT.

With Shine realizing those green eyes,
        Her face lifts like the SUN.

She grows a smile on her face
        That could not be UNDONE.

SHINE: But how can this be? You're a Glowie?
I thought you were a Glowie.

ALDIN: I am a Glowie! I'm still not so sure what happened. I have to tell you something though, and you have to keep it a secret, and please believe me when I tell you.

SHINE: I can do that, you can trust me.

ALDIN: Okay, well, I was in the mushroom field last night, and underneath one of the mushrooms, I found a golden scroll. When I opened it, I had this weird vision of the White Dog AZIZ and my father Tazan. It felt like I was there and watching the beginning of how everything started. My father, Tazan, fell down to the land with his followers and was forced into the Gloomy Night. I saw my father and his army in the shadows, stealing y'all's light from the Golden Day. Then the vision just went away and I was golden. I don't know how or why, but I believe my father is getting ready to try and take over the Golden Day. And I was chosen to stop him. Sounds crazy, right?

SHINE: No, that doesn't sound crazy at all. Actually, it kind of makes a lot of sense. Come follow me, I have something I want to show you.

Shine grabs Aldin by the hand
And takes him off to a distant PLACE
Meanwhile in the Gloomy Night,
Something very frightening AWAITS.

TAZAN: Come, you Glowies! Hurry, hurry, come get your new spray! After you get a taste of your new glow, I need you all to gather in front of my throne. I have some great and amazing news to tell you! WyUlle, come to me!

WyUlle: Yes, sire. You called me?

Tazan: Take a seat to the right of my throne.

WyUlle's heart immediately starts POUNDING.

To sit on the right side of Tazan's throne
Means your position in his kingdom is truly OUTSTANDING.

With all the Glowies in front
                                  And gathered TOGETHER,

Tazan begins speaking nothing but lies,
                      And just from the power of his tongue,
          Causes the order of a Glowie's life
                To be SEVERED.

Tazan: It breaks my heart having to tell you all this, but Aldin, my son, has betrayed us! He has stolen some of the new brew of spray and has joined forces with the Golden Ones!

He has deceived them all into believing that I, Tazan, am using you Glowies to take over the Golden Day! He has convinced them to steal and destroy our Gloomy Night and to take down our great kingdom that we have worked so long and hard to build!

We must rise up, my Glowies, and protect our way of life! We must become an army and wage war upon the Golden Ones before they have a chance to strike us! We must attack now and fast to catch them off guard!

Now go, my Glowies! Douse yourselves in SPRAY!
Feel the true power of your GLOW!
Let it gift you and use it as a weapon!

Forge this KINGDOM into a mighty FORTRESS! We have until the moon is at its highest peak, and then it will be time! Let's go to work, my Glowies! Work like you have never worked before! Work, work, work, build, and create! This shall be the last GOLDEN DAY they shall ever remember!

        With all of the Glowies
        Now hard at WORK

    Their minds overtaken with hatred and anger
        They start to REVERT

Back to their old ways of rebellion and desire to HURT
        Led blindly by Tazan
        Their hearts become CURSED

Taking up their new forms
                From this poison they call SPRAY
    Igniting a malicious evil inside
  All the Glowies start to wickedly PLAY
From sharp claws to giant BRUTES
        To crazed smiles
      And jagged TOOTHS
Lost in destruction
        They run wild
                In a strange LOOP

    Showing off their newfound weapons to each other
    And working harder than ever BEFORE

      Tazan seems pleased with his army
But in his black heart
                It'll never settle
    Until he has MORE

    TAZAN: WyUlle, come!

WyUlle: Yes, sire, what do you need?

Tazan: Go fetch me the four Witches. I need
their new glow to cast a storm.

WyUlle: Yes, sire, right away.

Back in the Golden Day,
  Aldin and Shine have reached the distant PLACE.

Both sitting next to the pond of bluest water,
  Shine takes a deep breath
And reveals something she's always wanted to SAY.

Shine: I know none of this makes sense, and I
know we just met, but I feel so comfortable with
you. Like I've known you my whole life.

Aldin: No lie, I'm feeling the exact same way.

Shine: My dad used to bring me out here when I was a little
girl. He used to tell me these extraordinary stories, which I
always thought he made up. I never felt like I fit in anywhere. It
was hard to make friends. I was so different from everyone, so
I kind of stayed to myself. Never felt like I belonged anywhere,
but my dad would always tell me that it's because I'm special.
He would bring me out here and tell me stories of how one
day I'll become a queen! That Aziz created me with a light
inside that would outshine the sun! Stories about how one
day, when I'm older, I'll be loved by everyone! That I'll meet
a boy and fall in love. He would tell me that Aziz has such a
great purpose for my life and that's why I feel the way I do.
That Aziz created me differently in that way because of how
much he loved me. My dad would also tell me stories of a man
who was sent from Aziz, a man that would bring magic and
do all sorts of amazing things. He said he would move the

sun to shine over everything in the land. That he would bring
golden statues to life. That he would do the most incredible
thing of all, and rapture all the people as one and bring them
home to Aziz in the clouds. After my dad would tell me these
stories, he would tell me to look into the bluest water with
him. Then he would always say the same words every time.

SHINE'S DAD'S VOICE: You see that girl right there in the water?
That girl is the greatest blessing I have ever received in my life.
You have brightened up my whole world since the day I saw
you and held you in my arms. That's why I named you Shine.

SHINE: Then he would turn my face towards his and say…

SHINE'S DAD'S VOICE: I love you so much, and
I know one day, Shine, you will brighten up
everyone's world just how you've done mine.

SHINE: He always believed this water had magic powers. That a
touch of its wetness would wash away all bad feelings inside,
keeping your heart pure, honest, and hopeful. That if you
ever lose sight of who you are, it will always restore you back
to your true self and remind you of how special you are.

ALDIN: Wow, I'm not really sure what to say. It sounds like your
dad really loves you, though. I'm sure he's an amazing person.

SHINE: Yeah, sorry if I bored you with that. I was
never able to tell anyone that before. And yeah, he was
taken a long time ago. I guess he needed him more
up there with him than I did down here with me.

ALDIN: I'm so sorry to hear that, and no, you
didn't bore me. I loved listening to you.

SHINE: He-he, yeah?

Glow to Gold

ALDIN: Of course. So do you believe in
the stories he would tell you?

SHINE: Ahh, no, not really. I just always felt like he
was telling me them to help cheer me up, but that's
one reason why I told you about all that. I never
truly believed in his stories until I met you.

ALDIN: Really, and why is that?

SHINE: Because for the first time in my life, I feel
like I do belong and that I do have a purpose.

ALDIN: Well, I'm glad I was able to help out, and for
the first time in my life, I finally feel as if I belong and
have a purpose. So what do you think about the water?
Do you think it really holds such magical powers?

SHINE: Ha-ha, umm, I don't know. I stick my hands in it every
time I come, but I never felt anything different or seen it
do anything. It does make me smile and remember my dad
and how he was always trying to lift my spirit back up.

ALDIN: Hmm, I believe it has powers. I think your
dad was right about everything he's told you, but
then again, maybe all anything takes is just the
power of believing in it for it to become true.

Then Aldin reaches his hand to the water of BLUEST,
Not sure what to expect,
But he never felt it was FOOLISH.

As soon as his fingers feel the slightest TOUCH,
He evaporates into thin air,
Leaving behind nothing but a cloud of gold DUST.

Shine: Aldin? Aldin? Where did you go?

Being zipped through time
And placed back into the Mushroom FIELD,
Aldin slowly awakens,
Unsure if it was all just a dream
Or if it was REAL.
With not being gold
And glowing like he did BEFORE,
He stands up and says…

ALDIN: That was such an intense dream,
I wish there was MORE.
Where did my spray go? I know I didn't leave it anywhere. Oh well, I should probably head back now.

Walking through the old rotten bushes
And past all the tall dead TREES,

Aldin sees something very odd with the kingdom:
Every Glowie is bound in some form of ghostly CHAINS.

Gasping at the SIGHT
And noticing the moon is turning blood red that NIGHT,

The memories of his dream come back,
And he says the words…

ALDIN: Oh no, this can't be RIGHT.

Aldin doesn't KNOW,
But Greeby and Sfary are right BELOW.

They're practicing their new glow of weapons,
Putting on quite a goofy SHOW.

Glow to Gold

Sfary: Grr, ahhh, grrrr!

Greeby: No, dude, that's not it. You're not doing it intimidating enough. You have to feel it.

Sfary: Oh yeah, like you can do any better?

Greeby: Uhm, umm. Ahhhhh, ha-ha-ha, hehe, slickempop!

Sfary: Uhh, ahh! I'm shaking. Ha-ha. You were so right, that was so much better. Not!

Greeby: Oh shut it! You're just jealous that I'm more frightening than you are.

From a slip on a STICK,
Aldin falls QUICK,

Landing right in front of Greeby and Sfary.
They jump into each other's arms with a scream
So terrifyingly SICK.

Greeby and Sfary: Ahh, ahh, ehhh, ahhhh!
Aldin?

Greeby and Sfary,
Looking at each other with such EMBARRASSMENT,

Quickly jump away
And pretend like that didn't just HAPPEN.

Aldin: Oh hey, guys, ha-ha. What are you two up to?

Greeby: Aldin the Betrayer! I didn't think you were dumb enough to come back.

Adam

SFARY: Maybe the Golden Ones sent him back to spy!
Huh, what are you doing sneaking around?

GREEBY: Trying to gather information to
save your poor little Golden Ones?

ALDIN: What are you guys talking about?

GREEBY: As if you don't know. Tazan told us everything, and
your new eyes of blue show the proof that he was right. Come
on, Sfary, let's capture this betrayer and bring him to Tazan.

Aldin, in a panic,
He throws dirt in their FACES.

Running off into the dark wilderness,
He quickly ESCAPES.

Enraged in anger,
Greeby and Sfary SHOUT:

GREEBY: We will find you, Aldin the Betrayer!

SFARY: And when we do, Tazan will lock you away forever!
And you'll never get OUT!

Aldin, hiding away in a secret cave,
He starts feeling safe and SOUND.

While Greeby and Sfary are on their way
To tell Tazan what they have FOUND.

GREEBY AND SFARY: Tazan, Tazan!

TAZAN: What do you two want?

Glow to Gold

GREEBY: We found Aldin in the woods sneaking around.

SFARY: He ran off into the dark wilderness.

Tazan, gripping them both with such strong MIGHT,
Pulls them closer and closer,
Squeezing them tighter than TIGHT.

TAZAN: And you didn't stop him!

WYULLE: It's okay, Father. Let me go; I know where to find him.

Tazan lets go with a face of DISGUST.
Greeby and Sfary rush away,
Sobbing and FUSSED.

TAZAN: Go, WyUlle. Bring him to the
Brew Factory. I'll meet you there.

WYULLE: Yes, sire. I won't let you down.

Sitting all alone in the cave,
Aldin begins to realize it was all REAL
And not
Just a DREAM.

That if he is going to put a stop to Tazan,
He will need himself a TEAM.

Aldin: Okay, okay, Aldin, think. What do I do? Shine, I have to make my way back to her! She's the only one who would believe the truth. We have to warn the Golden Ones, but how do I get back to her? I'm not golden anymore. Maybe I can find her by the Great Tree where we met. I so hope she's there, waiting for me.

WyUlle: Hey, Aldin.

Aldin: WyUlle!

WyUlle: What is up with your eyes, brother?

Aldin: I don't know, I'm not sure how to explain. So much has happened. I know our father has told everyone I have betrayed them, but it's not true.

WyUlle: It's okay, brother, do not fear. I believe you. Father is off on a hunt this way looking for you. I'm glad I was able to find you first, but we have to get moving. If Father finds you, there's no telling what he would do.

Aldin: You really believe me? I would never betray anyone.

WyUlle: You are my brother, Aldin. I know you wouldn't lie to me.

Aldin: Oh WyUlle, you're a great brother. Thank you for being on my side.

WyUlle: What kind of brother would I be if I wasn't? Now come on, we have to move. Follow me. I will take you to a place where you'll be safe, and then we can figure this all out together. Let's go.

At this moment in the Golden Day,
Shine is at the Great Tree where she sits and WAITS,

Hoping that her long-lost Glowie will come back
After watching him so suddenly disappear
From her FACE.

SHINE: Oh Aldin, what happened? Where did you go? I hope you come back to the place we first met. I know you will, and I'll be here waiting for you. No matter how long it takes.

BRIGHT: Shine, are you really going to sit here hoping to see that disgusting Glowie again?

SHINE: He's nothing like you think. He's amazing and smart. He's, oh my gosh, he's so handsome. And that smile, he-he, he has such a gentle heart.

BRIGHT: Okay, well, I'm going to go. And seriously, Shine, a Glowie? You're better than that. What could a worthless, disgusting Glowie ever give you that a Golden One can't? Oh wait, that's right, nothing! Because Glowies are nothing! They're just filth! They're so far beneath us it's not even funny. I hate to see you waste your time like this, but I guess you're just going to have to learn your lesson. Come on, Light, let's get out of here.

SHINE: You're wrong, you'll see! This one is different, made just for me.

BRIGHT: Whatevs!

SHINE: Come on, Aldin. I know you. Don't let me down.

While Shine sits and waits,
An unexpected destiny is COMING.

A fate set for the Golden Day,
So ruthless and cruel,
Will have the Golden Ones captured
And the rest endlessly RUNNING.

Deep in the Gloomy Night,
The blood moon is on the RISE.

And WyUlle is leading his brother Aldin
Right into a most hurtful SURPRISE.

Straight into the Brew Factory,
Aldin is played right into Tazan's HANDS.
A discovery will be made shortly after
That will allow Aldin to lay ruins
To Tazan's PLANS.

WyUlle: Come on, brother, inside the
Brew Factory you'll be safe.

Once inside the factory,
The door is slammed SHUT.

In front stand Tazan and four Witches.
Aldin looks at his brother with sadness
And says the word
Aldin: BUT.

Tazan: Nice to see you again, Aldin. Tell me, how
does it feel to have betrayed your own family?

Aldin: Brother, how could you do this? You set me up!

WyUlle: *Brother*? How dare you ever call me brother again! What is a brother that lies? What is a brother that can't be trusted? You are not my brother; you are nothing to me but a pool of Glowie waste! I hope you're happy with your deceitful betrayal. For now, you must watch as we destroy everything that still allows your rotten, diseased heart to still beat.

Glow to Gold

Tazan: Now that son is going to grow up and make me proud. As for you, Aldin, you're the son that will bring joy to my face as I burn down that new beloved light you have found into ashes and waste!

> Tazan leans in close,
> Whispering into Aldin's EAR.

> Tazan speaks in such a low voice,
> Making sure no one around can HEAR.

Tazan: Well done, my boy, the Pond of Bluest Water suits you well. I was counting on you to find it. I knew touching it would send you right back here to me, giving all the Glowies compelling evidence that you have betrayed them. Did you really believe you could defeat me? If only you would have stayed on my side. I am the ruler; I am the highest and mighty. My throne will be lifted beyond the Clouds of Siri, and when I do, you will fall with the rest of those precious Golden Ones. Remember where you came from, boy. The Glowies worship me; they are mine to command. What a fool you are to ever think they would choose you over me.

> With an extreme amount of anger and hurt,
> Aldin's flame grows **BRIGHTER,**

> Scorching Tazan's right eye,
> Making it look like molten lava and FIRE.

> With such a painful SCREAM,
> Tazan gets nasty and MEAN.

> He chains Aldin up center stage
> For all the Glowies to SEE.

Aldin looks out at the Glowies,
                 Seeing them all bound in ghostly CHAINS.
    He watches them all mindlessly working,
        Suffering from invisible PAINS.

TAZAN: All my Glowies, give me your attention!
I bring to you that wretched backstabber!

GLOWIES: Boo!
Send him to the Fire of Night!
No, exile him to the Darkest of the Night!
Yeah, exile!
Exile! Exile! Exile!

TAZAN: Ha-ha-ha. Exile it shall be, but first bring out the four Witches, WyUlle! He must watch our chaos and destruction! It's time, my Glowies, get ready to fight! Witches, use the power of your glow to cast a storm over the Golden Day. Transform and disguise my son WyUlle to take the form of Aldin here, and make sure he can see everything that WyUlle sees.

ALDIN: No, you can't do this!

TAZAN: It's too late; it's already done. Let's go, Glowies, set up formation in the shadows! When I say attack, let's scatter and leave nothing left with light!

Nice look WYULLE, just like your brother. Now you go out first and find that one thing Aldin fell in love with so much.

WYULLE: Yes, sire. I won't let you down.

TAZAN: Any last words from my used-to-be son?

ALDIN: Light will always outshine the dark!

Glow to Gold

TAZAN: Aha, did Aziz tell you that? You
should've chosen more powerful words.

ALDIN: It's true, and after I'm done with you, you'll
need more than just a few stitches for that eye!

Tazan's face falls,
And anger sets IN.
He heads off to the shadows
To watch his hostile takeover BEGIN.

The four witches join together,
Becoming stuck in a TRANCE,
Brewing up a gruesome storm in the Golden Day.
The Golden Ones stand no CHANCE.

WyUlle, in the form of Aldin,
Steps under the shadow of the Great TREE.

Shine, overtaken with joy, shouts out

SHINE: Hey, Aldin, I knew you'd come! Hey, Aldin, it's ME!

WYULLE: Umm—hi?

SHINE: What's wrong with you? Why are your eyes yellow?

Sneaking from behind the Great Tree,
Tazan comes to MEET.
Through his natural nature of DECEIT,
He thinks this will bring forth Aldin's
DEFEAT.

TAZAN: Well done, Aldin. I knew sending you here to find
the most precious and brightest light would work.

Adam

SHINE: What do you mean?

TAZAN: Aldin never told you? To tear down
this Golden Day, we had to find the greatest of
light and destroy it. That is you, my dear.

SHINE: Look at me and tell me that's not true.

WYULLE: Every word of it's true. What
are you going to do about it?

SHINE: I can't believe you! You lied to me straight
to my face! I trusted you! I hate you, Aldin! My
friends were right; you're nothing but filth!

Aldin, watching this through the eyes of his BROTHER,
Filled with such anger and hurt
                 And painful tears,
                                   Cries out...

ALDIN: No, Shine, don't believe them, they're lying!
That's not me, that's my evil father and BROTHER!

Tazan, feeling satisfied,
And black clouds cause the disappearance of the SUN.

Tazan looks at Shine, saying,
TAZAN: Dear girl, a strong storm is
coming. If I were you, I'd RUN.

Shine takes off running,
Overwhelmed and hurt with painful TEARS.

All Golden Ones had no knowledge
Of a war brewing NEAR.

Glow to Gold

But for the first time on the Golden Day, there is a storm,
And they are all hiding

In FEAR.

TAZAN: WyUlle, take Greeby and Sfary, go back, and send
Aldin into exile. Make sure he's never seen again!

WYULLE: Yes, sire, as you command.

TAZAN: Are you ready, my Glowies? Attack!

Out from the shadows
And into the STORM,

An army of Glowies covers their land like a blanket,
Shattering all gold,
Dimming all light to the color black,
And leaving all the Golden Ones' hearts

TORN

With WyUlle on his way
To abide by the will of his FATHER,
Aldin is deep in thought
On how the power of light could end the SLAUGHTER.
WyUlle shows up
With his new pals Greeby and SFARY,
Dragging Aldin by his chains
Into an exile so SCARY.

ALDIN: Don't do this, you guys; you don't know what you're doing. WyUlle, listen to me. Dad is just using you, can't you see that? He doesn't care about anybody but himself. He's using all of us; all he wants is to become mightier than Aziz. He's causing all this terror and horror because of pure jealousy!

WyUlle: Shut up, Aldin! You're the jealous one. For years I've had to sit on the side and watch as you were Dad's favorite. "Aldin, you're my image," "Aldin, you sit to the right of my throne," all *Aldin, Aldin, Aldin*! Well, not anymore! Now it's me, WyUlle. I sit to his right, I'm the one he calls to, and I am his image and prized possession now! Me, me, me, not you! You are the one that's jealous! You couldn't stand to see me becoming greater and mightier than you! So you betrayed us just to tear that apart? Well, I'm not letting you get in the way anymore! You let your pride and jealousy of my greatness be your downfall, my brother. Now you will live the rest of your days in exile for what you have done!

Aldin: WyUlle, my brother, please! Seek the truth and let go of this poisonous anger! What's corrupting your mind?

WyUlle: Quit with your lies and betrayal! This is your end. Do you have any last words?

Aldin: Light will always outshine the dark.

WyUlle: Aha, isn't that the same thing you told Dad? You're so pathetic!

Aldin: It's true, and WyUlle?

WyUlle: Yes?

Aldin: You're just like Father, maybe even more rotten and heartless.

WyUlle: Errr—you will know what rotting is soon enough!

WyUlle leaves in a rush,
Heart filled with HATRED,

Leaving Greeby and Sfary behind.
        They slowly leave Aldin,
                Feeling sad and wanting their old ways
                      to be changed and WASTED.

        Aldin, all alone
        In the darkest of NIGHT,
        Shouts out…

        ALDIN: Hello, anybody there?

Then takes a deep breath and closes his EYES.

        Back in the Golden Day,
All Glowies, still fighting in endless RAGE,
The light from the sun starts shining through,
        And the storm begins to DISSIPATE.

        Leaving their land in ruins,
    The Glowies take up their PRISONERS,

Bringing them all to the Gloomy Night,
        And as they cross over,
               Away their light WITHERS.

        The few Golden Ones left
        Walk around to see everything DAMAGED.

They begin to lose all hope in their salvation,
        Puzzled,
Wondering why they never received a warning or MESSAGE.

        The Golden Castle,
    Being the only place left STANDING,

Inside, Shine helplessly cries,
 Heart shattered into pieces,
  Her light shrunken down to a flame of a candle
And proceeds to keep FADING.

SHINE: Why did this happen?
I don't UNDERSTAND.
 Aziz, I need your help.
  Please give me your HAND.
 How could I be so FOOLISH,
Giving my heart away to this Glowie
 Whose only intent is to use IT?
  Please, I need your guidance.
  Please show me a WAY.
My heart can no longer bear this pain.
 Did I do something wrong?
 Is this how I must PAY?

 With Shine's faith,
  hope,
 And love DEPLETING,

A handsome little Golden fella walks in
 And gives her just what she's NEEDING.

 Blinding: Shine, is that you?

Shine wipes away her tears
 And turns around to SEE.
 It is a Golden boy named Blinding,
 And he is holding out a KEY.

 SHINE: Blinding?

 BLINDING: Yes, it's me. Are you okay? Come here.

Glow to Gold

Wrapped in each other's arms,
They both gain some COMFORT,
Still devastated by the storm
That brought lightning and THUNDER.

BLINDING: I'm so glad you're okay. I thought
you were captured with your friends.

SHINE: Everyone was captured, and it's my entire fault!

BLINDING: No, no, it's not your fault. Don't say that, and
there are still a few of us left. Look at me, Shine, it's
going to be okay, and none of this was anyone's fault.

Using his hands,
He wipes and dries up her EYES,
Making that little flame of light
Grow brighter INSIDE.

BLINDING: You have to be strong right now, okay? For
the sake of our people, not all hope is lost. I mean, we're
still here and all needing each other more than ever right
now. You're a tough girl, Shine; you have to be strong
for us and for yourself. You think you can do that?

SHINE: Yes, yes, I can do that. Thank
you for being here, Blinding.

BLINDING: Anytime, Shine, I'll always be here for you. I also
have this key for you. Your dad told me to give it to you
when the time is right, and I'm pretty sure now, after all that
just happened today, is the right time to give it to you.

SHINE: My dad gave this to you? What is it for?

Adam

BLINDING: No clue. He said you would know what to do with it. I'm going to be with the others and give you some time to think. Are you sure you're going to be okay?

SHINE: Yes, I'm going to be okay. Thank you.

BLINDING: Always my pleasure, Shine. I'll be back in a moment to come check on you. Stay tough.

With a cheerful spirit,
                     A smile,
                                      A GRIN,
He leaves her with a key,
    A secret to be unfolded, and a mystery to BEGIN.

               Shine, deep in thought,
    Trying to remember everything her dad has ever SAID,
A memory comes to mind
               Of a quote he hung
                                    Above his BED:

The key to salvation
Lays in the heart of the LAND.

Knowing this was the clue to point the way,
     She tries hard to UNDERSTAND.

        Slipping off into a dream,
She's standing in the Golden Days of OLD.

      Watching Aziz in the clouds,
He pours down the first sight of GOLD.

      Taking the shape of a heart,
     It sank into the GROUND.

Glow to Gold

A beam of light shot inside,
>>Locking away a victor's CROWN.

>Hearing a bark,
>Shine is suddenly AWAKE.
A little white dog named Q-Pit
>>Is licking her FACE.

>SHINE: Ha-ha-ha, oh my gosh, you are so cute. Where did you come from?

>Q-PIT: Bark, bark, huhuhuhuhuhu, bark.

>SHINE: Ha-ha, oh yeah, would you like to help us find where this key goes?

>Q-PIT: Huhuhuhuhu, bark, bark.

SHINE: Hmmmm, I think I know where to start looking. Come on—hey! Where are you going? Slow down! You're supposed to be following me. You little hyper-fluff ball of cuteness. Wait for me!

>Deep in the darkest of night,
>Aldin is sitting in EXILE,
Feeling like a failure
>>And having no more reasons to SMILE.

>After keeping his faith in the light,
>He gives up, losing himself in CONFUSION.

Then something magical happens:
>His chains float up and then they are LOOSENED.
>Amazed by what he SEES,
>Aldin looks up to AZIZ.

    Feeling sorry for losing faith in the light,
He knows in his heart
      That it was him above
          Who has set him FREE.

ALDIN: Thank you, Aziz, thank you, but what do I do now?

      Aldin looks around.
      All he can see is BLACK.

His glow gives off three feet of light,
      But it is just pure darkness after THAT.

      Aldin, wandering in different directions,
        Goes to take a STEP.

Then his body gets frozen in a force field,
    And he hears something in the darkness that CREPT.

ALDIN: Ahhh—what's going on? Who's there?

      Floating through the darkness,
       Aldin urges to FLEE.
Grunting and moaning,
      But he cannot break FREE.

    ALDIN: Okay, this really isn't funny. You can put me down now. It would be super cool to tell me who you are, and how you're doing this?

Then all of a sudden,
      Aldin is stopped
        And spun like a TWISTER.

He hears the voice of a man
And listens to him WHISPER.

Exiled Man: That's him, that's the one. I told you two he would come one day. Yes! I know you thought I was crazy, but now there's proof. No, not proof that I'm crazy. Okay. Wow, that's a little too far. No, he doesn't look that wimpy, and no, you can't eat him. What do you mean he looks too dumb to have a brain? Ha-ha, yes, he does have that problem, doesn't he? Okay, okay, enough! Shush! Bring him closer now so he can see.

Aldin, very CONFUSED,
Has the goofiest face to SHOW.

Brought into a small *cave*,
He makes it all GLOW.

What Aldin saw
And what Aldin SEEN

Was a man from the old Golden Days
And two little strange creatures of GREEN.

Exiled Man: Surprise! Oh, yeah, you were right. I can see it now, he totally does.

Aldin: Uhhmmm, hi. You see what?

Exiled Man: Ha-ha, nothing. Well, come here, don't be shy. Uhhh, give me a hug. So tell me, is she more beautiful than ever? I bet she's all grown up now and looking just like her mother. Whoa, I miss her. But hey! I bet you've been having quite the adventure. Busting into the kingdom like a hero! "There shall be no mercy!" Taking out all the bad Glowies like *boom-boom, pow-pow*. Saving the damsel in distress, "Oh, thank you, you saved me!" All the Golden Ones cheering you on like you're their savior. "Oh yes, you're our savior!" And now coming here to rescue us. Must've been exciting, huh?

ALDIN: Oh no. I'm not really sure what you're talking about. How long have you been out here?

EXILED MAN: No? What do you mean *no*? Of course, you know, why else would you be here? Oh, no, don't you start with the "I told you so's." Yeah, well, I might just be a little crazy, but you're stuck out here with me, aren't you? Okay, yeah, yeah, yeah, keep telling yourself that. Now shush it. Well? Why are you here?

ALDIN: So many reasons, long story short. I was forced into exile by the Glowies because my dad convinced them that I was a betrayer, but my dad is the one that…

EXILED MAN: Get out!

ALDIN: But, I—

EXILED MAN: Out, you're not the one! No, not right now, I don't want to hear it. Please, just leave it alone. I'm not in the mood for you to tell me. Wait a minute. You really think so? You believe that too? You two aren't just messing with me, are you? Okay, okay, maybe. Let me see. Hey, you! Come back here, I need to see something.

Aldin turns around
And heads back toward THEM.

The three were patiently waiting,
Standing before HIM.
As he got closer
And entered the CAVE,

Glow to Gold

All three of them noticed
        That his eyes are from the pond of bluest water
                He GAVE.

        All three were struck,
        With their minds stuck in AWE.

After spending countless years in exile,
        The one they've been waiting for
                Was him after ALL.

EXILED MAN: You really are the one! Ha-ha, come here, give me another hug! Ha-ha, do you know what this means?

ALDIN: No, what does it mean?

EXILED MAN: It means we're going home, back to the Golden Day. Ha-ha!

ALDIN: But how?

EXILED MAN: What do you mean, "but how"? You're how. You're going to bring us back. Woah! Get ready, my friends, I'm coming, Shine! Daddy's on his way!

ALDIN: Hold on! You're Shine's father?

EXILED MAN: Well, yeah, I thought you knew that?

ALDIN: No, I had no idea, to be honest. I have no idea about anything you've been talking about.

EXILED MAN: Huh, you two might have been right about that brain comment earlier. So what do you know?

ALDIN: I know right before I got sent here, my father Tazan sent his army of Glowies to take over the Golden Day.

EXILED MAN: So your father is Tazan? And what is your name?

ALDIN: Yes, and my name is Aldin.

EXILED MAN: Okay, so let me get this right. You're Aldin, son of Tazan?

ALDIN: Yes.

EXILED MAN: Okay, makes sense. And you're telling me there has been no butt-kicking of the Glowies?

ALDIN: Nope.

EXILED MAN: Uhhhhhmmmm, oh. So you're telling me that right before you got here, Tazan had just put together an army to try and take over the Golden Day?

ALDIN: Yes, that's what I'm telling you.

EXILED MAN: Oh boy! Yes, that's exactly what that means. Nope, it looks like we're going to have to be here a little while longer.

ALDIN: What? What is it, what's wrong?

EXILED MAN: I'm afraid to tell you this, Mr. Aldin, but I fear we are only at the beginning. You'll have a lot longer to go before you'll be able to defeat Tazan and put an end to his destruction.

ALDIN: Hmmm, okay! Well, what do we do now, or what should I be doing?

EXILED MAN: Well, we can't save us and take us back to the Golden Day until it's restored to its former glory. So I guess we're going to do the only thing we can do.

ALDIN: And that is?

EXILED MAN: We train!

ALDIN: Train? What kind of training can we do here?

Song: "Glow in the Dark"

Artist: Jason Gray
(The song plays as the training takes place)

VERSE 1
The two green creatures are shaking Aldin back and forth with their force field. Aldin's face shows stress, making his heart start to glow. Shine's dad puts his hand inside Aldin's side, squeezing his heart and making Aldin's flames grow out, blowing over the two green creatures.

VERSE 2
Then Shine's dad glows a dim light and is no longer hidden in the dark. He holds his nose and blows out air to pop his ears, making him glow dim. Then he points to Aldin, gesturing for him to try.

VERSE 3
Aldin looks at him funny but then tries it. When he does, the flames from his glow start burning intensely fast, and Shine's dad nods with a smile.

VERSE 4
Shine's dad closes his eyes and flexes, straining. Then his heart starts to light up and burns like a flame. Shine's dad gestures to Aldin to try it. Aldin closes his eyes, flexes, and strains. His glow goes out, leaving only a glowing red heart. Then his glow comes back, and he still has his eyes closed, flexing and straining. His heart blinks into a golden light and then back to a glowing red heart. Shine's dad shakes his head and points to Aldin's heart.

VERSE 5

Aldin holds his nose and blows, making his flames burn intensely fast. Shine's dad closes his eyes, flexes, and strains, growing his light heart of flame brighter and a little bigger. They both look at each other, laughing.

VERSE 6

Aldin looks at Shine's dad's heart and then at his flames with a frown, lowering his head. Shine's dad shakes his head, waves his hands no, and then points to his glow of flames, smiling and giving him two thumbs-up.

VERSE 7

Shine's dad kicks Aldin's legs together and straightens Aldin's arms out. He puts his hand into his back, squeezing his heart again, making flames shoot out from his hands, feet, and head, forming a cross. The two green creatures on each end now under Aldin's flaming light show a face of excitement.

VERSE 8

Shine's dad grabs his nose. Aldin and he both blow, making Shine's dad stay in the same dim light and Aldin's flames burn intensely fast as they laugh.

VERSE 9

The two green creatures are in the light of Aldin's glow, holding their noses, but nothing happens. Then Aldin does it, making his flames grow intensely fast and laughing at them. While looking down and shaking their heads in disappointment, Shine's dad puts a hand on each of their heads, still straining and shaking, making them both light up green for a second. They jump in the air, waving their arms up and showing a look of woe on their faces. Then Aldin closes his eyes, strains, and flexes, making his heart light up into a flame. Aldin smiles, then his flame of heart burns out back into a red glow heart, and he shrieks in frustration. Shine's dad holds out his hand, tilting it back and forth with an almost-there look on his face.

VERSE 10
Aldin is forced down to the ground by the two green creatures' force fields, making his glow of flames go out. Then Aldin breaks the force field with an intense blast of burning flames while rising up. It blows the two green creatures away and blows out Shine's dad's dim light, making him hidden in the dark again. Aldin's heart is now a golden light of flame, and Shine's dad dims back up in a glow and is holding his nose, blowing. Aldin looks at Shine's dad, smiling, and nods at him. Shine's dad smiles back, shaking his head yes, claps his hands, and gives him a thumbs-up.

VERSE 11
Aldin is thrown far off into the darkness of exile by the two green creatures' force field. Aldin then starts looking around intensely, straining his eyes, glowing his flames taller, and burning his heart of golden flame brighter until his eyes light up into a blue flame and now Aldin can see in the dark. Aldin walks up and finds the two green creatures hiding. When found, both green creatures look at him with wide eyes and a surprised look on their faces.

VERSE 12
Aldin walks up to Shine's dad, smiling, flames growing bigger, golden-hearted flame burning bright, and his eyes glowing a blue flame. Shine's dad gives him a big smile and nods his head. Aldin puts his hand on Shine's dad's heart and restores his golden form to him. Then he removes his hand and Shine's dad goes back to being a dim glow.

VERSE 13
All four start laughing and giving each other high fives.

(Matthew 5:16)
Aldin, now back in his original form,
He's learned how to keep his powers harnessed INSIDE.

Knowing his purpose is to save the Golden Ones,
His first step in doing so
Is returning to the Gloomy Night
And cutting his TIES.

Aldin, excited,
Feeling happy and fulfilled with himself,
He is ready to take on that TASK.

But he has some questions for the man in exile
That he is in dire need to ASK.

Exiled Man: Well done, Mr. Aldin, that was extraordinary, what you did.

Aldin: Yeah, it was, wasn't it? But how did you know I was able to do all that? How did you know it was possible?

Exiled Man: Because I was able to wield powers just like that, Mr. Aldin. Although that was a long time ago.

Aldin: Really? And what happened? How did you end up here?

Exiled Man: Well, a long time ago, many years back, the Golden Ones were in trouble and in danger of Tazan destroying them for good. So I did what I had to do to save them. I sacrificed the greatness of light with love for them, locking it away in the Golden Day. It would keep the Golden Ones covered in light by the sun, always bringing them hope and protection. For my sacrifice to fulfill the promise I made to the Golden Ones, I had to give myself over to Tazan. He banished me here into the darkest of nights for exile, and I've been here ever since.

ALDIN: Wow! You must have really loved the Golden Ones to give up your own life for them.

EXILED MAN: I did indeed, Mr. Aldin, but most of all, I could never see anything that awful happen to my sweet, beautiful, and loving Shine. I will always do what I need to do to keep her safe, but don't you go thinking I don't have a backup plan now? During the sacrifice of my greatest light, I took a piece of it and put it in Shine. That way, she may always have a direct connection to Aziz, and by holding that little piece of power, she'll be able to guide the one called forward in the right direction, fulfilling the prophecies and returning me back home.

ALDIN: No wonder you always told her such incredible stories growing up, and they were all real! I'm so sorry all this happened to such a good man like yourself.

EXILED MAN: Ahhh, no biggie, ha. It had to happen that way. But you need to get going. You have a lot of work to do, and time is getting short. Here, take these two with you. They might be a little different, ha-ha. But they are very loyal and will always have your back. They'll always keep you protected by warning you of any danger coming.

ALDIN: But what about you? I can't just let you stay out here alone!

EXILED MAN: Don't you worry about me, Mr. Aldin. I assure you, I'll be just fine. You just stay focused and get your job done. I'm counting on you to look after my little girl. Now go on, get going, and don't you look back when you leave.

ALDIN: Okay, I sure will. Thank you for everything. Tell me this before I leave, though, please? Who were you—or are you? What's your name?

EXILED MAN: I am the greatest of light and whoever believes in me shall have everlasting light, my name is The Sun of Flames.

ALDIN: I believe in you, Sun of Flames. I am so grateful to have met you.

EXILED MAN: I am as well to meet you, Aldin. See you soon, and you two behave!

ALDIN: I'll be back sooner than you think! You can count on that.

As Aldin walks away,
Never to look back AGAIN,

The exiled man,
Son of Flames,
Bursts into a Golden man
With golden glittery flames,
Eyes of blue flames,
And ascends up into the clouds where everything BEGAN.

Greeby and Sfary were there,
Watching from a DISTANCE.

Both their jaws dropped
And eyes widened
From what they have just **WITNESSED**.

SFARY: Ummm…Greeby… Did you just see that?

GREEBY: I did, Sfary, I did.

SFARY: Oh man! Are we bad Glowies, Greeby? Please tell me we are not bad Glowies!

Both Greeby and Sfary look at each
other with emotions of PAIN.
Then, grabbing and holding each other,
Crying out in tears,
They both chant out words of the SAME.

Greeby and Sfary: We're bad Glowies! Ahhh, ahhh, sniffle, we are so sorry, Aldin! Ah, ah, ah.

Still on the Golden Day,
Shine is on an adventure to find where the key FITS.

Losing sight of the little dog Q-Pit,
She heads to the center of the land
Where she believes the lock SITS.

In the middle of the land
Stands a golden statue of a man named Sun of FLAMES.

Shine, so certain in her mind,
Believes this is where the lock to the key REMAINS.

Shine: Okay, I know it has to be somewhere around here. Nope, nope…not here. Uhh, not here either…nope, nothing. I'm sure it is, though. That dream showed the middle of the land. Maybe this statue opens up a secret doorway. Yay, that's it! Uhhh…errr…come on, you statue of a man! Do something…uhhherrr.

Shine pulls and tugs,
But nothing is HAPPENING.

Getting worn out and frustrated,
She hears someone LAUGHING.

Blinding: Ha-ha-ha! Shine, what in the
Golden Day are you doing?

Glow to Gold

Exhausted, she sits,
Blowing her hair out of her FACE.

She looks up to see Blinding
And says…

SHINE: How often did you ever come out here to this PLACE?

BLINDING: Umm, not that often. Why?

Out of her pocket,
She holds up a KEY,

Then mumbles the words…

SHINE: I'm trying to find the lock for this.
I figured this is where it'd BE.

BLINDING: Oh, yeah, well you look like you're in a better mood.

SHINE: Ehh, not really. Just trying to keep my mind busy. You haven't seen a little white dog anywhere, have you?

BLINDING: A little white dog?

SHINE: Yeah, adorable little thing. It just showed up in the castle earlier, and then took off. I swear it was trying to get me to follow him, but he disappeared. Uhh, I'm so tired of that.

BLINDING: Tired of what? Are you okay? You know stress can cause illusions. You've been through a lot today; we all have. Maybe it'll be best if you lay down and take a nap. I mean, you're out here pushing and pulling on statues, talking about a little white dog that no one's ever seen.

SHINE: I'm tired of being led on for nothing!
And what, you think I'm crazy?

BLINDING: No, not thinking that. I was just saying.

SHINE: Well, come on, I'll prove it to you.
Let's go find him; his name is Q-Pit.

BLINDING: Lead the way, I guess. You know where this little Q-Pit might be?

SHINE: Nope, no idea. He took off to the right after leaving the castle. So we'll start there.

BLINDING: Well, okay. I'm following you.

While looking around the land,
Blinding notices something odd while searching for Q-PIT.

The Glowies didn't come for the Golden Day to be destroyed;
They came for it to be LOOTED.

SHINE: Q-Pit, oh Q-Pit, where are you, boy? Mauh, mauh, mauh, come here, Q-Pit, mauh, mauh, mauh!

BLINDING: Shine, hold up a second, come here.

SHINE: Yeah, what is it?

BLINDING: I don't think the Glowies were here just to destroy everything. I think they were looking for something.

SHINE: Something like what?

BLINDING: Not entirely sure, but whatever it was,
I bet that key you have has something to do with
it. We need to find where that key goes.

SHINE: Well, duh, what do you think I've been trying to do?

BLINDING: Call upon your imaginary friend.

SHINE: Oh, funny. Ha-ha-ha. Q-Pit's real, you'll see.

BLINDING: I'm sure he is. Well, come on, let's go find Q-Pit then.

Both Shine and Blinding look around for Q-Pit
But he seems nowhere to be SEEN.

They call out his name along sidewalks,
By houses,
And even in the STREETS.

Then Shine and Blinding walk near some Golden Ones
Who are all still in mourning for the LIGHT.

Blinding goes up to each of them, asking a question:
Have you seen a little dog named Q-Pit?
He's small and WHITE.

GOLDEN ONES: A dog, are you mad?
A dog named Q-Pit? You must be stoopit.
You're worried about a dog during this crisis?
A dog, there's no dog in this land. What's making you see a dog?
Oh, yeah, a little dog, small and white, named Q-Pit? No, I've
never seen a dog. Crazy. Is something wrong with you?

BLINDING: Shine, I'm trying to believe you, I really am.
But don't you think you could've just imagined that you
saw a dog? I mean, I imagine things all the time. Like

one day, I thought I saw a tree that was golden, but it was just my foot in the way, covering up the tree.

Shine: No, I'm not imagining this, okay!

Blinding: Okay, I believe you. I'm going to sit down for a bit. I'll be right over here on this bench next to this old, worn-down wagon.

Shine: I'll sit with you. I need a break too.

Blinding: You believe everything's going to be okay? That everyone who was captured will return somehow, and the Golden Day will be back like it used to be again?

Shine: I believe everything's going to be fine and that it'll be better than it ever was!

Blinding: Ha, yeah, I sure hope so. But don't you—

Q-Pit: Bark, bark ahahahahahaha.

Shine: Q-Pit! Oh, you sweet boy, I knew I would find you. And where were you, huh? Did you find where or what this key goes to?

Q-Pit: Bark, bark, ahahahahaha, bark.

Blinding: Oh wow, there really is a little white dog named Q-Pit. Well, hey there, little fella, we've been looking…

Q-Pit: Bark, bark, grrr, errr!

Blinding: Ahh, I don't think he likes me very much.

Shine: Oh, Q-Pit, come here. That's a good boy. Don't worry about him; he's harmless.

Glow to Gold

Q-Pit: Ahahahaahaha, slickem, slickem, bark, bark.

Shine: What is it, Q-Pit, did you find something?

Q-Pit: Bark, bark, ahahahaaha.

Blinding: I think he's trying to tell us to look under this wagon. Here, let's move this hay and take a look.

Blinding grabs handfuls of HAY,
                      He digs through and tosses it AWAY.

While clearing a path,
He slips down a HOLE.

And under his feet
Is a door of silver and GOLD.

Blinding: Shine, Shine, we found it!

Q-Pit: Grrr, grrrr, bark.

Blinding: Okay, okay, you found it, geez!

Q-Pit: Ahahahahahaha.

Shine: Great job, Q-Pit. Now let's find out what's inside.

Slipping the key in the lock,
The doors open up like a GATE.

Inside is a staircase leading down into darkness,
                      And a quote above
That will test their belief
And their *faith*.

Adam

Quote:
There is no light too big
Just as there is no light too small
But the only way to enter inside, is to have no light at all
Hidden in the darkness ahead, hides life's greatest secret
And only the one who was given the eyes of
truth, wields the power to reveal it

BLINDING: Yeah, I don't get it. So how do we get inside?

SHINE: It sounds to me like there's only one person that can. Must have no light and have eyes of truth.

BLINDING: What does that even mean? Who would have no light and eyes of truth? This just doesn't make any sense. I'm going to try and go in.

SHINE: Be careful, you know you can't go in the dark.

Slow and steady,
Blinding makes his way IN.

His light casts out the dark,
Only to show an empty room of stone and a piece of old TIN.

BLINDING: There's nothing in here, Shine!
Come see, just some old tin.

Shine makes her way DOWN,
    Already knowing that nothing would be FOUND.

She puzzles through names in her head,
But none seem to fit the quote's SOUND.

BLINDING: Well, what shall we do now?

SHINE: Maybe head back to the town and ask the ones that are left? See if they know anything that would help?

BLINDING: Yeah, just not sure if it's a good idea to be talking about it. We can't risk the Glowies hearing about what we found.

SHINE: We have to do something. I know whatever is in there will save us.

BLINDING: You're right. I mean, what else do we
have to lose? Let's go see who can help.

Coming out of the room
And back into the light of DAY,

Shine looks around for Q-Pit,
But it seems again
He has run AWAY.

SHINE: Q-Pit, come here, boy! Mauh,
mauh, mauh, mauh, really, again?

Shine and Blinding cover the door back up with hay,
Then make their way back to TOWN.
While Aldin and his two new green friends
Arrive in the Gloomy Night,
Peeking at the sight of it from behind a tall MOUND,

Aldin watches dimly lit Golden Ones
Being trapped in cages of LIGHTNING.

With some new machine stealing more of their light,
It is making Tazan more FRIGHTENING.

The two green creatures look at each other,
Very scared and AFRAID.

Aldin then tells them…
ALDIN: Don't worry, ok? We're going to come up with a
plan, and for what Tazan has done, he surely will PAY.

Aldin turns around,
Kneeling out of sight and closing his EYES.

Thinking really hard about what to do,

Glow to Gold 63

He hears a sound a distance in front of him—
A sound of a faint CRY.

Aldin sharpens his eyes,
Looking into the distance
And outlining the DARK.

He spots Greeby and Sfary,
They're hiding in a cave,
Trying to ignite inside themselves a light SPARK.

Aldin puts out his glow,
He becomes UNSEEN.

Tells the two green creatures

ALDIN: Stay put and watch ME.

He walks toward Greeby and Sfary,
Being very quiet and SNEAKY.

Once he's behind them,
He glows back his flames and says…

ALDIN: What are you doing? Did you miss ME?

They both jump away
With a sheer look of TERROR,

Screaming such girly screams
And hopping in place, looking FAIRER.

GREEBY AND SFARY: We're sorry we turned our backs on you. We didn't know, please forgive us.

ALDIN: It's okay, guys, relax. I saw you
two spying on me in exile.

SFARY: How do you know that?

ALDIN: Because I was just watching you both
trying to make light grow inside you.

GREEBY: Yeah, but it's not working.

SFARY: How did you do it, Aldin? Teach
us and let us join you to help.

ALDIN: I could really use you guys, so yes, please join me. As
for the light, you're doing it right. You just need to believe
more in yourselves, then it will work, but you have to believe.

GREEBY: Yes, sir, sir Aldin, sir!

SFARY: And what do you need us to do?

GREEBY: Yeah, I'm ready.

SFARY: I'm ready too.

ALDIN: Well, to start, let me introduce you to
my two new friends. Ok, you two, come out and
meet my two best pals, Greeby and Sfary.

Stepping from behind two dead TREES,
 Out pop two little creatures of GREEN.

GREEBY: Ahh, ahh! Eww, what in the
world of Glowies are those?

Glow to Gold

SFARY: Ha-ha, look how weird-looking they are, Greeby.

With a grin on the two green creatures' FACES,
They pick them both up in a force field,
Bouncing them around and shaking them in different PLACES.

Then letting them go in the air
To fall on their FACES.

The two creatures of green wipe off their
hands and nod their HEADS,
Giving them both a look like, say it
again and you both are DEAD.

GREEBY: Okay, sorry, Glowiezz!

SFARY: Yeah, talk about sensitive.

ALDIN: Ha-ha, oh yeah, you all will get along great. We have a nice little team here, friends. Now the first thing we must do is free the imprisoned Golden Ones without getting caught or having them noticed they're escaping.

GREEBY: And how are you suggesting we do that?

ALDIN: Well, I'm kind of thinking you
two would be my distraction.

GREEBY AND SFARY: Distraction!

All five huddle together,
 And Aldin takes the lead
  To lay out the PLANS.

Aldin, trying to form something that looks like
he's everywhere at once in the LAND.

Adam

ALDIN: Okay, here's what we're going to do. I have no idea what we're going to do. All I know is that I can go unseen and let the Golden Ones out from the cage. I just need you two, Greeby and Sfary, to distract Tazan and WyUlle. These two can assist you with that as well, but we still need to break up the witches.

GREEBY: Yeah, uh, I can get WyUlle to go on the outskirts with me. That would take care of him.

ALDIN: Okay, and can one of you go with him and contain him there? Good, and after he's contained, Sfary, I'll need you to come back and deal with the witches.

SFARY: So you're saying I have to be the one to deal with Tazan?

ALDIN: Only for a moment. When Greeby gets back, you'll swap, and then you would go bother the witches and make them lose their trance.

SFARY: And how do you want me to do that?

ALDIN: Good question. This one right here will make sure you do what needs to be done.

GREEBY: Oh, Glowiezzz, I see this going all kinds of wrong.

SFARY: Uh, yeah, I'm not feeling too good about this plan.

GREEBY: Nope, nope.

ALDIN: All you need to do is just keep them away from the cages and their attention… What is that? Yes, that would be perfect. Are you sure you'll keep me safe that long? Then that's a plan!

Glow to Gold

GREEBY: What's the plan? We totally missed what just happened.

SFARY: Yeah, can you explain that?

ALDIN: You two are going to let the Golden Ones out, and I'll take care of the rest. Do you think you can handle that?

SFARY: Oh yes, that sounds a lot safer.

GREEBY: A lot safer!

ALDIN: Then let's do this. Everyone ready?

GREEBY: No, definitely not ready for this, and look at Sfary. He's freaking out.

SFARY: Everything's going to be fine. Everything's going to be fine. Everything's going to be fine.

ALDIN: Look at me, guys! They still believe you're one of them. Just act normal. All you have to do is, when the coast is clear, just open the cages. Simple.

SFARY: Simple, real simple. Just open the cages. I can do this.

GREEBY: I'll be with you, Sfary. We got this together.

ALDIN: Alright, let's go!

Everyone shakes off the nerves,
Then peeks over some bushes to get a LOOK.

What they saw when peeking over changed everything,
And the plans they made were quickly SHOOK.

Tazan had transformed into a serpent

Adam

From all the light he had consumed WITHIN.

There's only little time left now to save the Golden Ones
Before Tazan stores them all in his personal DEN.

ALDIN: Okay, we need to act now! Wait until I have Tazan's attention, then you two help Greeby and Sfary take out the Glowies guarding the cages. Once they're taken out, you two get the Golden Ones free. Got it?

GREEBY: Yes, but Aldin, I mean I have your back no matter what. I'm just having this really awful feeling inside that something bad is going to happen.

SFARY: Yeah, I'm having the same feeling, but if you're ultimately sure about it, just say the word. We're ready.

ALDIN: No, you're right, guys. Y'all just stay here. This is something I have to do.

With Aldin on his way,
Doing something either really stupid or BRAVE

The other four are left behind,
Left with an insatiable hunger to help,
        Something in dire need to CRAVE.

All standing with a feeling that they are HELPLESS,
They muster up great courage inside
To do something
        That's SELFLESS.

GREEBY: Come here, you guys. We can't let Aldin do this alone. We need to do something to help.

SFARY: I agree, it wouldn't be right if we didn't.

Glow to Gold

The two green creatures nod with a yes gesture.
They all come together close,
Talking in a soft WHISPER.

Aldin is now unseen after putting out his glow.
He's sneaking right up to Tazan,
Having a calm anger,
But ready to cause chaos
Like a TWISTER.

As he gets closer,
Tazan starts sniffing with his tongue.
He knows that Aldin is NEAR.

Then Tazan speaks out
Into the AIR.

TAZAN: I know you're here. Umm, you smell
of great fear. Show yourself to me! How were
you able to get out of exile, I wonder?

Tazan starts slithering to the front of the stage.
Aldin bursts onto the scene with his glow of FLAMES.

Standing tall and putting off a horrific fright,
Both eager to put an end to these GAMES.

ALDIN: Right here, Tazan!

TAZAN: Ahh, there you are. How noble of you to
have come and bear witness to this magnificent
transformation about to take place.

Aldin: Stop this right now, Tazan!

TAZAN: Hahaha, oh dear child, but it's already begun.
On with the transformation, my Glowies, hahaha!

Witches dance,
Cages MOVE.

The new machine sucks in Golden Ones,
Spitting out Glowies
That are conformed to a dreadful GROVE.

Tazan is LAUGHING,
Golden lights SHATTERING.

The team of four show up in the back,
Just in time to see what's HAPPENING.

Aldin screams,
His flames ARISE,

Burning taller and faster,
With blue flames as EYES.

His heart is a Golden FLAME,
Filled with anger,
Rage,
And PAIN.
Tazan's face will surely change
When Aldin shouts his NAME.

Aldin: Tazan!

TAZAN: No, how could this be?

All around are shocked and DAZED.
Greeby and Sfary shout out…

Glow to Gold

GREEBY AND SFARY: No freaking Glowie WAY!

The two green creatures frantically WAVE.
Greeby and Sfary look at each other, confused, and say…

GREEBY AND SFARY: What did they just SAY?

The two creatures of green slap their
faces and shake their heads.
One takes Greeby and Sfary AWAY,
While the other goes to help Aldin SLAY.

Greeby and Sfary are put in a force field
And handed to the Glowie guards as a MARK.
Then the green creatures make them TALK.

GREEBY AND SFARY: Hurry, hurry! There are Golden Ones sneaking in that way. There, the backside of the Forest of Dark.

The Glowie guards start to RUN,
Taking with them a Glowie army of a TON.

GREEBY: Well, that was easy.

SFARY: Yeah, ha-ha, that was kinda fun.

The green creature nods with a SMILE,
And Aldin feels a force field wrapping him up
And believes it's time to fight with STYLE.

His flames glow out,
And now UNSEEN,

He's moved into the middle of the witches.
Glowing back his flames,
So tall,

Fast,
And MEAN.

The power of Aldin's glow
Throws the witches to the FLOOR.

The transformation ritual stops,
And the machine turning the Golden Ones to Glowies
Works no MORE.

TAZAN: No, stop him! WyUlle, where are all my Glowies?

WYULLE: I don't know, Father.

TAZAN: Then find them now!

With a sweeping of Tazan's tail,
He knocks WyUlle AWAY.

Locking eyes on Aldin,
He hunts him down like PREY.

Aldin burns in and out of glow,
He's zipped to the left,
Then to the RIGHT.

Unable to keep up with such quick movements,
Tazan stumbles now to FIGHT.

Greeby,
Sfary,
And the creatures of green
Open up the cages' GATE.

WyUlle and the army of Glowies show up, swarming the cage,
And only Bright and Light manage to ESCAPE.

Glow to Gold

GREEBY AND SFARY: Go, go, run! Take them to
the Great Tree! Ahh, ahhh, WyUlle!

GREEBY: Aren't you looking very Glowie tonight.

SFARY: Yeah, did you do something different with
your face? You're looking very angry that way.

WYULLE: Get them!

GREEBY AND SFARY: Ahh, ahh!

Greeby and Sfary run away,
Arms flailing up in the AIR.

The Glowie army takes off after them,
While WyUlle looks at the cage of Golden Ones
With such an evil STARE.
Aldin zipping from the front and zipping from the BACK,
Tazan ties himself in a knot
And now can't ATTACK.

Tazan tries to untangle himself,
Using all his MIGHT.

Aldin and the green creature disappear,
Leaving just a golden-hearted flame right in Tazan's SIGHT.

The Glowie army comes up with WyUlle
And the four witches STAND.

Tazan, enraged with fury, speaks out…

TAZAN: You have all let me down! This
shall never happen AGAIN!

Adam

Tazan gets untied and free,
Slithering up tall,
He gains his COMPOSURE.

Then says to all…

Tazan: I don't need an army of useless Glowies!
I need an army of SOLDIERS!

All Glowies in fear,
Scared
And SHOOK

Kneel down, waiting for Tazan's command
As he creepily LOOKS.

Tazan: Now back to work! We're not finished here yet. Turn these unfortunate Golden Ones into Glowies. Move it, work, work, work!

Witches resume dancing,
Machine on full BLAST.

The rest of the Golden Ones are turned into Glowies,
And Tazan's army begins building FAST.

Now at the Great Tree,
Under the shadow,
All five are back UNITED.

Having Bright and Light among them,
Shine and Blinding are soon to be SIGHTED.

Greeby: Whew, that was crazy!

Sfary: I didn't think we were going to make it out of there.

Glow to Gold

ALDIN: Yeah, but we didn't accomplish anything.
Tazan still has the Golden Ones and is building an
even bigger army. All that was just pointless.

The two green creatures pat Aldin on the back
And gesture to keep his head UP.

Bright and Light smile with joy,
Jumping up and down, saying…

BRIGHT: I can't believe you two Glowies have saved
US! You are my tall Glowie hero, thank you!

GREEBY: No problem. It was easy to do for you.

Then the Golden Girl, Light
Bends to Sfary and kisses him on the CHEEK.

Sfary's face glows a bright red.
Then after a moment, he SPEAKS.

SFARY: Aww shucks. Thanks. He-he.
You kiss one before, go more.

Light's eyebrow rose
And a tilt of her HEAD.

Greeby and Bright look at Sfary,
Confused at what he just SAID.

Light just smiles
And kisses Sfary's other CHEEK.

Sfary's face glows even brighter,
Then he faints, trying desperately to SPEAK.

BRIGHT: Light, look, there's Shine. Shine, Shine!

ALDIN: Shine!

Aldin looks up,
Seeing pure amazement and BEAUTY.

A smile grows on his face,
And his world seems less CONFUSING.

Bright and Light cross over to the Golden Day.
They both turn back GOLDEN.

Waving goodbye to Greeby and Sfary,
They both just stand FROZEN.

BRIGHT: Yay, girl. We're gold again!
High five, we must tell Shine.

Shine and Blinding are in the midst of the TOWN,
Looking for Golden Ones to see if they
know anything about what
They have FOUND.

They ask her,
They ask HIM,
Not knowing where to BEGIN.

The question asked is THIS…

SHINE AND BLINDING: Do you know anything about a locked gate, leading into a room with a riddle, or what the gift of life IS?

And all the Golden Ones just reply back:

GOLDEN ONES: I've never heard of such a thing, my FRIENDS.

Glow to Gold

Then Shine stands up in front,
With a loud voice casting over all of the PEOPLE.

She is the representation of the church,
And the Golden Castle is their comfort and their STEEPLE.

SHINE: Okay, Golden Ones, can I have your attention, please! I know we're all hurting—our fathers and mothers, sons and daughters, brothers and sisters—all captured by Tazan and his army of Glowies and left us all devastated! But this is not a time to give up or walk around hopeless! We still have each other, and that's what gives us hope! It's time we all band together and form an alliance! Blinding and I have found a room leading to our salvation! The only way to get our families back is by becoming unified! Don't just have faith in me and my words, but have faith in one another, have faith in Aziz! For his love will save us all! Now are you with me, Golden Ones?

GOLDEN ONES: Yes, we're with you!
United we stand, divided we fall!
Let's get our families back, Golden Ones!
It's time to let our light SHINE!
Yea, whuu, yea!

Shine: Alright then, follow this way! We have a riddle to solve.

BRIGHT: Wow, girl! Whatever it is, she's got it!

Bright and Light start yelling out Shine's NAME.
Shine looks over to see who's calling her.
Stunned by who she sees,
Her eyes can't seem to EXPLAIN.

SHINE: Bright and Light! Oh my gosh, you're okay! I thought you both had been captured. What happened?

BRIGHT: Crazy story, girl! Like OMG, first off, we got picked up by these creepy, disgusting Glowies, and they threw us in this cage. Then all of our lights went out and they put us in the middle of the Glomie Night! It was so scary, girl! Light and I were both like, "This is the end. We're goners!" Then this big noisy metal thing started turning the Golden Ones into Glowies. Light and I just held each other and cried, like, OMG, Shine. Worst time of my life. Then like, out of nowhere, these two big, strong, handsome Glowies came up and saved us. Shine, girl, you have to save the rest. You're the only one that can do it! Girl power!

All the girls lift their hands together in the AIR,
Wiggling and touching fingers
Like they just don't CARE.

SHINE: Okay, come on, girls! Blinding! Lead the way to the room!

Meanwhile, under the great tree,
The team of five is wondering where they are.

GREEBY: So what do we do now?

ALDIN: I don't know, Greeby. But if I haven't said it yet, thank you guys for helping me. I probably would've never made it out there if it wasn't for y'all.

SFARY: No problem, Aldin. That's what friends are for.

GREEBY: Well, we can't go back now.

ALDIN: No, that's exactly what we should do.

GREEBY: Uhm, excuse me?

Glow to Gold

ALDIN: Yeah, we need to spy on them and find
out when they plan on attacking again.

SFARY: We don't have to stir up any trouble this time, do we?

ALDIN: No, not at all, just need to find out what
their plans are so we can be ready.

GREEBY: Then let's go spy.

The two green creatures shake with fear as they go off to SPY.
Meanwhile, in the Golden Day,
All the Golden Ones are about to meet a very strange GUY.

BLINDING: We're almost there. It's right
underneath that wagon. Hey, who's that?

The Golden Ones look,
But it's a man they've never SEEN.

Which is strange in the Golden Day,
Everyone knows everyone,
And to not be known brings CURIOSITY.

SPARK: Hello, my fellow Golden Ones. Isn't it a lovely day?

BLINDING: Who are you? Why have we never seen you before?

SHINE: Yeah, start talking, mister!

SPARK: I assure you, there's no need to be alarmed. My name
is Sparkling Flare, but you all may just call me Spark.

SHINE: Okay, Sparky! And why is it that no one knows you?

SPARK: Uhm, it's Spark. And I live beyond the Pond
of Bluest Water. You don't know me because no
Golden One has ever gone beyond that pond, and I've
never needed to come here to this town before.

BLINDING: So why are you coming here now?

Golden Ones: Yeah, very strange!
How do we know you're telling the truth?
He could be an impostor, ahhhh!

SPARK: Calm down, everyone, please, please calm down.
Shine, my child, have you seen my dog anywhere? Q-Pit.

SHINE: Q-Pit's your dog? Hey, how did you know my name?

SPARK: Simply, he told me. He is my dog
after all, he tells me everything.

SHINE: Well, no, I haven't seen him. It's okay, everyone, there's
no need to fear! This man is honest about what he says.

SPARK: Aren't you all here to find something?
Don't let me stand in the way of that, go on.

Shine looks at him
With a feeling she knows this man SPARK.

Then she turns away to reveal this riddle,
A riddle about light and DARK.

SHINE: If anyone knows anything about what this riddle
means, please come forth and tell us. I believe what is in
here could save the Golden Day and bring back all our
captured Golden Ones. Listen up, here is the riddle!

Glow to Gold

SHINE: There is no light too big,
Just as there is no light too small,
But the only way to enter inside is to have no light at all.
Hiding in the darkness ahead lies life's greatest secret,
And only the one who was given Eyes of Truth
Wields the power to reveal it.

Does anyone know how or who could answer this?

No Golden Ones say a WORD.
The only sound that is made
Is the chirping of a BIRD.

Then out of the silence,
They hear a GASP.

It is the unknown man Spark,
And he is going to answer
What was just ASKED.

SPARK: Hmm, the Sun of Flames…

SHINE AND BLINDING: The Sun of Flames?

GOLDEN ONES: Did he just say the Sun of Flames?
Yes, he did.
The Sun of Flames what?

SPARK: Yes, the Sun of Flames. This is his riddle.
He must have left it here as a reminder. After so
many years, this is where he chose to hide it.

SHINE: To hide what, life's greatest secret?

SPARK: Yes, but it's not much of a secret at
all. Life's greatest secret is LOVE!

Adam

SHINE: LOVE is life's greatest secret?

SPARK: Of course, my child, but that's not what's in here. Many years ago, when the Sun of Flames sacrificed himself to save all the Golden Ones, he found a way to harness the power of love and locked away his greatest light somewhere no one would find. Doing that allowed the Golden Day to always give its light and to always outshine the dark. The power of love is the greatest power in all the world. Love will always overcome and always conquer anything. You, my child, have found and unlocked the passageway to harnessing that power.

SHINE: But who is able to find his greatest light?

SPARK: That's all in the riddle, my child. My guess would be whoever was given the Eyes of Truth. That could be anyone. You know Aziz works in mysterious ways. You've made it this far, so I wouldn't give up hope just yet. I'm sure that person will be right in front of your eyes soon enough... It was a pleasure meeting you all! Never lose faith in the Golden Day! I will be back to be with you! Time is of the essence!

Q-PIT: Bark, bark, huhuhuhuhu.

BLINDING: Q-Pit!

SPARK: Oh Q-Pit, my boy. Are you ready to return home? I have a treat for you.

Q-PIT: Bark, uhuhuhhuuh.

SPARK: Blinding! Walk with me for a moment, would you?

Shine and the Golden Ones,
Unsure of what to do or how to ACT,
Walk back to the town.

With only faith,
Hope,
And love,
They form the greatest PACT.

BLINDING: Yes, sir, Mr. Spark…

SPARK: Please, just Spark.

BLINDING: Spark…

SPARK: Blinding, you are about to perform the most courageous of acts. I assure you, you will be rewarded tenfold for it. Please keep your feelings aside and let your faith, hope, and love conquer your fear. The greatest of lights is waiting for you on the other side.

BLINDING: What am I going to do?

SPARK: That doesn't matter. Be brave, Blinding. Now go with the others and lead them to victory.

BLINDING: Nice to meet you, Spark. You take care.

SPARK: My pleasure, Blinding.

Blinding heads back to town,
He's weirded out by the NEWS.

And in the middle of the Gloomy Night,
Tazan's army of Glowies is in formation under the MOON,
All paired in TWOS.

As the team of five is quietly WALKING,
Greeby and Sfary are continuously TALKING.

SFARY: We should have an awesome team name.

GREEBY: Like what?

SFARY: Like… Sfary's Glowie, Green, Hero team!

GREEBY: That's stupid.

SFARY: And you can come up with something better?

GREEBY: How about Team Sneaky Force, ha-ha…

    The two green creatures slap their faces
    And shake their heads in SHAME.

    Then Sfary whispers out loudly…

SFARY: Wow, that's super **LAME**…

ALDIN: How about Team SHHH, before
we get caught. Now quiet down.

SFARY: Sorry, Aldin, just figured we needed
an awesome name for ourselves.

ALDIN: Shh, we'll discuss that later. Come on.

Greeby and Sfary hide behind a big rock,
    And Aldin with the two creatures of green
               Kneel down behind a rotten LOG.

All trying to see the Glowie army,
    But they can't see anything through the thick,
                        Thick FOG.

ALDIN: I can barely see anything; we might need to get closer.

Glow to Gold

GREEBY: Can't you use your eye thing? Will that not work?

ALDIN: Good idea, Greeby. I can't believe
I forgot about that. Let me try.

Aldin looks down,
And by his feet is a mushroom of GOLD.

He notices writing on the top,
And he picks it up to read.
...LO AND BEHOLD...

Then Aldin looks up,
Seeing everyone plus the fog to be all GONE.

He hears Tazan's voice yelling...

TAZAN: Destroy my Glowies! The war is ON!

Then the Gloomy Night changes,
And Aldin is placed in the Golden DAY.

A storm brews up above,
And the Glowie army comes out from
the shadows ready to SLAY.

He watches as the Golden Ones stay STILL,
Standing strong together
And waiting for Tazan and his army to take the FIELD.

Behind the Golden Ones is a gray GATE.
There is a sign pointing to it saying,
Only you. Here waits your FATE.

When Aldin looks back to the Golden Ones,
They are all DEFEATED.

Then he sees Tazan holding Shine in his hand,
Slithering up to a new throne to be SEATED.

The storm in the Golden DAY
Stays stuck in the air like GLUE.

Tazan's throne sits in the middle of it,
And his eyes turn from red to BLUE.

Tazan sits in his throne,
And laughing so TALL

Tazan looks up to the sky and says…
TAZAN: Aziz the Almighty! Hahaha, now it's your turn to FALL.

Aldin, not believing what he's seeing,
Closes his eyes TIGHT.

Then he hears the voices of Greeby and Sfary…

GREEBY AND SFARY: Wake up, Aldin, wake up!

And then he feels a BITE.
Aldin then awakens,
Feeling one of the green creatures biting his ARM.

And when he opens his eyes,
Greeby and Sfary are right in his face,
Smiling with such CHARM.

Aldin shows a face of fright
And crawls back fast,
Stopped by a TREE.

Greeby and Sfary then speak out…

Glow to Gold

SFARY: What's wrong, Aldin, are you okay?

GREEBY: Yeah, you just fell over and went to SLEEP.

ALDIN: We have to get out of here now. We have to warn the Golden Ones. Tazan will stop at nothing until the Golden Day is destroyed and he sets up his new throne to Aziz… We have to move now. No time to waste.

All five, in a rush and panic,
Head straight to the shadow under the Great TREE,

Hoping to see some Golden Ones nearby
So they can warn them of what is soon to BE.
When they arrive,
There is nothing AROUND.

No sound to be heard,
And no Golden Ones to be FOUND.

Then out of nowhere,
They hear little FOOTSTEPS.

It is a little white dog,
That cute little Q-Pit.

ALDIN: Q-Pit! I can't believe it's you. Come here, boy!

Q-PIT: Bark, bark.

ALDIN: Hey, Q-Pit. Boy, am I happy to see you.

Q-PIT: Uhuhuhuhuh, bark, huhhuhuhuh.

GREEBY: Wow, even in the shadows this dog never loses his white color…

SFARY: That's so weird. What are you?
The two creatures of green, filled with joy,
Start smiling and DANCING,

Spinning in circles,
And silently CHANTING.

ALDIN: I need you to do something for
me, Q-Pit. It's very important.

Q-PIT: Bark, bark.

ALDIN: I need you to find Shine and get her to meet me here
under the Great Tree. Can you do that for me, boy? Huh?

Q-PIT: Bark, bark… bark.

ALDIN: That's a good boy. Thank you. Please hurry; it's urgent.

Q-Pit takes off,
Running so FAST.

All five are looking back at the Gloomy Night,
Hoping that the wait doesn't LAST.

In the town of the Golden Day,
Q-Pit comes rushing IN

Darting straight for Shine,
Wagging his tail with such a happy GRIN.

Q-PIT: Bark, bark, bark. Huhuhuhuhuh.

SHINE: Hey, boy! Awe, you are so adorable.
Are you happy to see me?

Glow to Gold

Q-Pit: Bark, bark!

Shine: I'm happy to see you too.

Q-Pit: Bark, huhuhuhhu.

Shine: Oh, you want me to follow you? Well, don't leave me this time, okay? Hey, girls, I'll be right back. Just make sure no one gets separated. You have to stay together.

Bright: But you're leaving?

Shine: I know, I'm sorry. I have to go; it seems important.

Q-Pit: Bark, huhuhuhuh.

Shine: I'm coming, I'm coming!

Bright: Okay, girl, whatevs! You better be careful though. And you better hurry back so I know you're okay! Light girl, when this is all done, you need to polish up.

Shine, trying to keep up,
Runs as fast as she CAN.

Then she spots Aldin under the shadow of the Great Tree,
And suddenly the pain from her broken
heart resurrects AGAIN.

Aldin: Good boy, Q-Pit. I knew you could do it.

Shine: Oh no! I can't go talk to him.

Q-Pit: Bark. Bark, bark. Bark.

Aldin, smiling,

Adam

So happy to see SHINE.

Inside, she's hurting bad,
    Knowing nothing can change what happened,
        That there is no REWIND.

SHINE: No! I can't. Hearing him talk would just break me.

ALDIN: What is she doing? Why is she just standing there?

Q-Pit takes off
Toward Shine he GOES.

When Q-Pit gets to her,
He starts nibbling at her ankles and TOES.

Shine: What are you doing, Q-Pit?

Q-Pit: Bark, bark.

Q-Pit spins in circles,
Gesturing her to FOLLOW.

Shine takes a deep breath,
But her heart's still filled with SORROW.

SHINE: Okay, Q-Pit, I trust you. If this is what you want me to do, then I guess I'll do it. Please don't let him hurt me again.

Q-PIT: Huhuhuhuhuh, bark.

Both head now
Toward the Great TREE.

Aldin is nervously waiting,
While Shine just wants to LEAVE.

Glow to Gold

As soon as they meet,
There's that same lock of EYES.

Aldin still feels that strong connection,
But Shine is losing sight of it
From all of the LIES.

GREEBY: What is happening right now?

SFARY: I think Aldin's in love. This should be good.

The two creatures of green
Bump Greeby and Sfary's heads TOGETHER.

Greeby and Sfary: Oh!

Then they drag them away
So Aldin and Shine can have a moment
of privacy to TREASURE.

ALDIN: I have to warn you, Shine. Tazan and…

SHINE: How could you? You lied to me. I trusted you, and you used me.

ALDIN: No, Shine, that wasn't me. That was my brother WyUlle! They tricked you! They only did that to hurt me. I'm sorry that happened, but you have to believe me.

SHINE: You hurt me deep, Aldin. How can I believe you when every time I see you, you're in a different form? First green eyes, then yellow, and now they're blue. Who are you? Every word you spoke has been a lie.

ALDIN: Shine, look at me! You know who I am.

SHINE: You just look bad, Aldin. Why do you keep playing with my heart?

ALDIN: I'm not, Shine. Please believe me. I would never do anything to harm you. All I've been wanting is to see you and talk with you. You have given my life such great meaning, and all I want is to be with you.

SHINE: How can I believe anything you say? I refuse to give in and fall into the same trap. You've already broken my heart. What more do you want?

ALDIN: I'm telling the truth, Shine. Tazan chained me up and forced me to watch him and my brother deceive you against me. Then I was thrown into exile. I've been trying my hardest to make it back to you. I can't stand living this life without you by my side. Also, I met your dad. He is such a great man. He loves you and is so proud of you, Shine.

SHINE: Why, why would you do that?

ALDIN: Do what?

SHINE: You are the worst, Aldin! You would really stoop that low to win my heart over by telling me that you met my father? My father's gone, Aldin! You are truly a monster! I feel so ashamed for ever wanting to know you. Is this what you wanted? To break me down into nothing? Well, I hope you're happy because you did it. Congrats!

ALDIN: No, Shine, stop! I'm telling you the truth, believe me! I'm not lying, I'm not trying to hurt you! But we're running out of time! I have to warn you that Tazan and his army are…

SHINE: Save it, Aldin! I'm done. I don't want to hear another word out of your mouth. Goodbye, Aldin. I mean, you can't

even cross over into the Golden Day. I guess that was just
another spell of deceit or your brother just playing tricks on me.

Aldin reaches into the Golden Day,
But his hand quickly BURNS.
Aldin pulls his hand back, hissing from the hurt,
And Shine says…

SHINE: And you're the one I gave my heart to. I'm so pathetic.

Then turning away, she quickly TURNS.

ALDIN: No, Shine! Please come back!

Aldin drops to his knees and says…

ALDIN: Why won't she believe me?

Aldin, very sad,
Loses his hope and just WISHES.

Greeby and Sfary
Talk with themselves in the DISTANCE.

GREEBY: Well, that was unexpected.

SFARY: Yeah, I thought they were going to start kissing.

The two creatures of green
Again bump their heads TOGETHER.

GREEBY AND SFARY: Oh!

Then they hear the sounds of footsteps
And feel a slight change in the WEATHER.

Aldin watches Shine walk away
And sees her losing her LIGHT,

Turning from gold to gray.
Then soon she will be black as NIGHT.

Shine, intensely crying,
Pours out tear after TEAR.

Blinding rushes to her aid
But is unable to bring her CHEER.

Aldin just sits there,
Seeing her fade away and forever be LOST.

He starts begging for it not to happen,
For his heart would surely be frozen in the FROST.

ALDIN: No, please no! Aziz, please, don't let this happen! I'm so sorry, please no! Please no! Please no! Aziz, please don't let me lose her, I'm so sorry!

Glow to Gold

Song by: Danny Gokey
Title: "Haven't Seen It Yet"
(This song plays while Aldin crosses over and saves Shine.)

VERSE 1
Aldin on his knees, head down, eyes closed, and hands together with his lips saying prayers.

VERSE 2
Shine's crying and Blinding's running up to her for comfort, but she pushes him away.

VERSE 3
Back to Aldin as he looks up, opening his eyes and dropping his arms down by his side, slouching to the ground and letting out a big sigh.

VERSE 4
Now to Shine, and she hugs Blinding tight, then begins crying onto his shoulder. Blinding holds her back tight and runs a hand through her hair.

VERSE 5
Now it shows the first time of Aldin and Shine meeting and her helping him up, then both jumping back away from each other. Then shows the scene of Aldin smiling at Shine, putting his hand in the water, disappearing, and her looking all around.
Aldin: I'm coming, Shine. I have faith Aziz will get me to you.
Aldin puts his hand in the light and takes it back out from the burn then shakes it off and toughens up his face.

VERSE 6
Aldin jumps through and crosses over into the Golden Day. Burning off his glow, he's now golden. He looks at his arms and body, checking it out. It shows Greeby, Sfary, and the two green creatures with their jaws dropped and eyes widened. Then Aldin balls his fist, making a gesture of "Yes, he did it."

VERSE 7
Aldin takes off running, looking at Shine up ahead in the distance. He's bumping into Golden Ones, jumping over bushes, and ducking under tree branches, trying his hardest to get to Shine.

VERSE 8
Shine, still crying, and Blinding is looking a little aggravated.

VERSE 9
Shine sees Aldin, all Golden, running toward her really fast. She lifts her head off Blinding's shoulder and stops crying, but still has tears running down her face, and she's fading to the color black.

VERSE 10
Now it shows the scene when Aldin finds the scroll and turns Golden. Then it shows Tazan and WyUlle as fake Aldin, deceiving Shine.

VERSE 11
Then back to Aldin running, and he trips to the ground right as he reaches up to Shine.

VERSE 12
Aldin stands up and dusts himself off, staring at Shine.

VERSE 13

Aldin grabs Shine by her hand and pulls her to him, staring eye to eye. Blinding backs up with hands in the air, confused.

VERSE 14
Aldin pulls Shine in close and kisses her. Her light comes back immediately, and she's Golden again. Then they both just look at each other, smiling.

VERSE 15
Aldin and Shine are now holding hands and running. They're spinning around, smiling at each other, and all the Golden Ones are shocked, seeing their love and happiness. But Aldin and Shine are acting like they're the only ones there, never losing eye contact.

VERSE 16
Blinding spots a girl in the town smiling at him, and he smiles back. Then he looks down at the ground shyly and kicks a rock.

VERSE 17
Blinding looks back up at her, and they lock eyes.

VERSE 18
In the Gloomy Night, a burst of light energy flows through, hitting all the Glowies. They all get pushed back a little, and Tazan looks to the sky, worried. Then it shows Aldin and Shine at the Great Tree, meeting up with Greeby, Sfary, and the two green creatures. The two green creatures just walk over to the Golden Day, and nothing happens—they're still just green, no change. Everyone looks at them like, "Really?" And they just shrug their shoulders. Then Aldin points to Greeby and Sfary, and the two green creatures start pulling them across. They jump into each other's arms, eyes closed, crying, scared, and screaming.

VERSE 19

When they cross over, they turn Golden. Opening
their eyes, they look at each other and jump away.
They both check each other out and themselves,
smiling, and then do a goofy handshake.

VERSE 20
Bright and Light pass by, and Greeby and Sfary run after them,
trying to hit on them. Greeby gets slapped by Bright, then
she takes his hand and skips away with him. Light kisses Sfary
on the cheek, and he turns red and faints. Light just looks at
him, and he's on the ground with a huge smile on his face.

VERSE 21
Shows Aldin and Shine smiling at one another.

VERSE 22
Blinding and the girl he locked eyes with
are both walking toward each other.

VERSE 23
Blinding and the girl meet up. Then Bright breaks through
between them, dragging Greeby on the ground behind her.
Blinding and the girl look at them, smile and giggle, then look
back at each other. Then it shows Sfary's face smiling while still
out cold, and then it shows the sun lighting up the whole scene.

The power of true love's KISS,
  Mending Shine's heart back together, and then it was FIXED.

With all of that PASSION,
    Doubt and fear were handed to love for SMASHING.
    Knowing the strength of them together,
    Soon the evil between their two worlds would
      be brought down CRASHING.

Aldin and Shine,

Now having an even deeper CONNECTION,

Are holding each other tight
With such great AFFECTION.

ALDIN: I'm so sorry.

SHINE: I am too.

Greeby and Sfary,
Amazed by their new FEATURES,

Forgot all about Bright and Light being around
And brought much laughter to the two green CREATURES.

SFARY: Whoa, hahaha! I feel so awesome!
Boom, boom, pow, pow! Ha-ha-ha!

GREEBY: I look so cool now, Sfary. Check
it out! Uhh, urgg, hauu, oh yeah!

BRIGHT: OMG, you're a jweeb! Did I really just fall for
a jweeb? Let's get out of here, Light, like now!

Bright and Light
Both walk AWAY,

But Light is still looking at Sfary
In the most adorable and loving WAY.

SFARY: Haha, you're a jweeb!

GREEBY: Na-uh. You are!

SFARY: No, you are!

GREEBY: Well, you're jweebier!

SFARY: Then you're jweebiest!

GREEBY AND SFARY: Aha-ha-ha!

Greeby and Sfary begin to WRESTLE,
    Both looking really goofy
        And both getting TANGLED.

    Then Greeby wraps Sfary up
    With his arms behind his HEAD.

    Sfary loses his breath,
    And his face turns blue and RED.

SFARY: Okay, you win. You're not a jweeb.

Greeby lets GO
        And backs up real SLOW.

SFARY: Huuuuuuu, gosh, you're so mean!

    Still holding each other
    Are Aldin and SHINE.

Then the two green creatures come up, gesturing
    That they're almost out of TIME.

ALDIN: Shine, I've been trying to warn you. Tazan and his army of Glowies are on their way to strike again, but this time he's coming to take over and destroy the Golden Day.

SHINE: How much time do we have?

ALDIN: Not enough. I'm sure he's on his way now.

SHINE: Then let's go round up the Golden Ones and get them ready for the war Tazan is bringing.

ALDIN: Shine, I had a vision of all the Golden Ones standing up to Tazan, and they were all destroyed. Is there somewhere safe they can all hide?

SHINE: I have a plan. Come on.

ALDIN: You four stay here. When Tazan and the Glowies get close, come to the town and let us know it's time to be ready. Thank you.

SFARY: Umm, he totally just ditched us, didn't he?

GREEBY: Yes, he did. I guess we're not as important as his new little golden girlfriend.

The two green creatures
Throw a rock at Greeby and Sfary's HEADS.

GREEBY AND SFARY: Oh! What was that for? Why do you two keep hitting us in the **HEAD**?

The two green creatures
Gesture to grow UP.

GREEBY: That's really funny, coming from someone that's the size of a baby **PUP**.

The two green creatures
Show their teeth and put their claws in the AIR.

Greeby and Sfary take off running, saying...

GREEBY AND SFARY: Okay, I'm sorry, we didn't mean it. We **SWEAR**! Ahh, this is so not **FAIR**!

Heading into the middle of town,
Aldin and Shine take the SPOTLIGHT.

Shine shouts out to all the Golden Ones…

SHINE: I need all women and children inside the Golden Castle, and I need all the men here to stay and **FIGHT**!

ALDIN: Please, Golden Ones, we have to move fast! Tazan and his Glowie army are on their way now! Are you ready for this?

SHINE: As ready as I can be, but Aldin, no matter what happens, we can't let Tazan or anyone from his army get to, or find, what's under that wagon.

ALDIN: What's under that wagon?

SHINE: No matter what, Aldin, you hear me! We lose if they find it.

ALDIN: I hear you, no matter what. But what is it?

SHINE: That's where the Greatest of Light is hidden.

ALDIN: The Greatest of Light? Shine, your dad!

Women and children in the Golden Castle,
Men on the field,
The Golden Ones SCATTER.

Greeby,
Sfary,
And the two green creatures come running,

Glow to Gold

Yelling out loud...
GREEBY AND SEARY: Aldin, Aldin! Tazan and his army are coming, and I've never seen him **MADDER**!

ALDIN: Okay, the storm isn't here yet, so we still have a moment. Shine, you and the Golden men try and take the fight towards the Pond of Bluest Water. My team and I will find the witches and take them out. No witches means no storm, and no storm means no Glowies or Tazan.

SHINE: What about my father? And yes, I heard; take the fight to the Pond of Bluest Water. You and your team, witches, but my father?

ALDIN: Awe, there's so much to tell, and I promise I will tell you when this is all over. The storm is coming! Now is just not the time. We need to split up. Give me your hand. Be careful out there, Shine. I love you. I'll see you soon.

SHINE: And I love you, Aldin. I know you'll come back to me.

The storm forms,
Covering the Sun and blocking the LIGHT,

Turning this beautiful Golden Day
Into a dark and weary NIGHT.

Aldin goes left, and Shine goes RIGHT.
Aldin takes the witches, and Shine takes the FIGHT.

Out from the shadows,
Into the STORM,
Tazan's army is soon to SWARM.
Thunder rolls and lightning FLASHES.
Through Tazan's eyes
Is all light burning down to ASHES.

TAZAN: Tonight is our night, my Glowies! Can you feel it, hahaha! We are not here to fight, my Glowies. We are here to stay! To build our new kingdom! This is our land, and when you go out there, don't just take it over. Plant your gloomy seed in the ground and destroy the Golden Day forever. Ha-ha-ha-ha!

While Tazan is laughing,
He gets hit in the back of the head by a STONE.

Looking like a fool now in front of his army,
He has a quick change in TONE.

TAZAN: Who threw that?

Popping out from a ROCK,
On time like a CLOCK,
Shine stands there, giving Tazan quite a SHOCK.

SHINE: So are you just going to stand there all night and talk or what?

TAZAN: Ahhh, get them! But she's mine!

SHINE: Uh, oh!

Shine moves fast;
She takes off RUNNING.

The Golden men see in the distance
A frightful Glowie army that is COMING.

On the other side of the storm,
The team of five are quietly SNEAKING,

Knowing Tazan has them hiding somewhere.
It's the witches they are SEEKING.

ALDIN: Do you guys know where the witches might
be? I can't seem to outline them anywhere.

GREEBY: Maybe they're still in the Gloomy Night.

ALDIN: No, they still have to be in sight of the storm.
What is the weakness of a Glowie? What is the
weakness of a Glowie? The weakness of a Glowie?

SFARY: What is that, Aldin? I can't hear you.

ALDIN: I think the witches might be in a
hole in the ground somewhere.

Greeby and Sfary: In a hole?

The two green creatures just shrug their SHOULDERS,
Then they point over by the Dark Forest
To two giant BOULDERS.

ALDIN: It's worth a shot. Let's go find out.

GREEBY: I can't believe we're back in our Glowie forms.

SFARY: Yeah, you dumb storm. We're taking you down.

Back to Shine and the Golden men,
And what's taking place on their SIDE.

All they can see of the Golden Ones now since the storm
Are just them fully gray,
With a dim-hearted light INSIDE.

SHINE: Okay, here they come. Everyone in positions!

GOLDEN MAN: We're all set, Shine!

SHINE: Good, I sure hope this works!

Tazan and his Glowie army arrive
To see Golden Ones spread out all over the LAND.

All the Glowies start to smile.
They start to laugh,
Grunt,
Stomp,
And wipe their HANDS.

TAZAN: Well, what are you all doing? They're
just sitting out there—attack!

Off the Glowies GO,
                                      Attacking swift and LOW,

Pouncing on the Golden Ones,
But it seems to be a magic SHOW.

GLOWIE: Ahh, urrr! Humm, what is this?

In the background, you hear Glowies SAY:

GLOWIES: HEY?
Hey, what's the big idea?
HEY?

A Glowie picks up a mirror
And sees his REFLECTION,

Then jumps back and screams
At an ugly INSPECTION.

GLOWIE: Ahhh!

Glow to Gold

Then the Glowie picks it back up
And looks AGAIN.

GLOWIE: Oh hey, that's me. Well, hi there,
good looking. How are you DOIN?

Tazan then screams in a GRUNT.

TAZAN: Urrrr!
So furious at the Glowie army in FRONT.

TAZAN: They're just mirrors, you IDIOTS!
They're tricking you, find them!

Tazan then drops to the ground,
Slithering on his belly.
He makes no SOUND.

Aldin and his team finally make it to the boulders,
And wouldn't you know it,
There's a hole to be FOUND.

SFARY: It sounds so angry out there.

ALDIN: Yeah, well, once we find these
witches, it'll put a stop to all that.

The two green creatures gesture
That they'll stay up TOP,

And that if anyone tries to intrude,
They'll make sure they STOP.
They ball their fists and punch their hands,
Showing that they're ready for ACTION.

Aldin, Greeby, and Sfary go inside the hole,

Ready to flush out the main ATTRACTION.

ALDIN: I only see two witches in here.
Where would the other two be?

As Aldin, Greeby, and Sfary get closer,
They bump into an invisible WALL.

The other two witches are sneaking
behind the two green creatures,
Very creepily they CRAWL.

One witch jumps on one green creature,
And the other on the SECOND.

The green creatures throw them off with a force field,
Then stand up in fighting position,
About to teach them a LESSON.

The two witches start throwing glowing balls of energy
With such slow, long STRIDES.

The two creatures of green catch them in a force field
And begin to toss them from side to SIDE.

Aldin puts his hand on the wall,
Then he closes his EYES.

A golden flame bursts from him for a split second,
Burning down the wall, then says…

ALDIN: Haha, nice TRY.

Greeby and Sfary fall back,
Shielding themselves from the LIGHT.

Glow to Gold

Then they both speak out in awe…

GREEBY and SFARY: Whoa!

SFARY: That was awesome!

GREEBY: RIGHT!

The two witches start throwing glowing balls of energy
As they're backing away.
Greeby and Sfary start laughing.

GREEBY AND SFARY: Hahahaha!

ALDIN: What is so funny right now?

GREEBY AND SFARY: We're Glowies, remember?
Uhumm, excuse us if you may.

Greeby and Sfary jump in front of the Glowie balls of energy,
Absorbing them INSIDE.

Then they start to grow big and tall like giants,
Laughing hysterically with such great PRIDE.

GREEBY: Hahahaha, yeah, you better run away!

SFARY: Haha, why so scared? We just want to play.

GREEBY AND SFARY: Ha-ha, he-he, ha!

The two witches look at each other,
Having a very evil SMILE.

Then they throw more glowing balls of energy,
Growing Greeby and Sfary so big

That they'll get stuck in the hole for a WHILE.

The two witches leave
With a smirk of GOODBYE.

Aldin slaps his face and shakes his head, saying with a grunt...

ALDIN: Uhh, you GUYS!

Greeby and Sfary look at each other,
Then they both just BLINK.

Aldin leaves them behind,
Knowing it would be a waste of time
Waiting for them to SHRINK.

SFARY: That did not work.

GREEBY: Yeah, I totally saw that going differently.

There's a moment of a long, awkward SILENCE,
Both their eyes wide open,
Having a look of shame on their faces for becoming so GIANT.

SFARY: We might be here for a while.

GREEBY: Definitely.

Above the hole,
The green creatures and the witches are still FIGHTING.

The other two witches join in,
And Aldin is right behind THEM.

On the side with Shine,
The Golden men stand out in the open for the Glowies to FIND.

When the Glowies find them all standing together,
They are surely SURPRISED.

GLOWIE: Ha-ha, there's nowhere for you to hide
now. You're right where we need you to be.

All the Glowies whisper to one another,
Then rush forward to take them out
with such wicked SCANDALS.

But as soon as the Glowies get close,
The Golden men pull out lit-up CANDLES.

GLOWIE: Whoa! Hey, easy with that. Someone could get hurt.

GOLDEN MAN: Back, you Glowie, back!

GLOWIE: Really, you actually think that could stop me?

The Glowie takes his hand
And puts the flame of the candle out between his FINGERS.

Then shaking his hand around from the burn, he says…

GLOWIE: I am strong and mighty! Not soft and WEAK, ha-ha!

All the Glowies then begin
Knocking down their candles
And putting out their LIGHT.

The Golden men try to stand tough
But are overcome by FRIGHT.

Shine is on the edge of a cliff,
Looking over to watch the BATTLE.

Her faith begins to slowly sink
As she watches the Glowie army herd up
the Golden men like CATTLE.

Shine: This is not good. Aldin, please hurry and stop this storm. That seems to be our only hope now. Wait, where did Tazan go?

Tazan rises from under the cliff.
He's looking mean and crazy TOO.

Face to face with Shine,
In a deep and vibrating voice, he says…

Tazan: BOO.

Shine falls back,
Frightened and scared.
She lets out a GASP.

Tazan smiles,
Closes his eyes,
Tilts his head up,
And begins to LAUGH.

Tazan: Hahahahaha!

Blinding, close by,
Watches with a tear in his EYE.

Thinking back to the conversation with Spark,
Suddenly he begins to REALIZE.

Blinding: I know what I have to do.

Shine, stuck frozen in FEAR,
As Tazan slowly draws NEAR.

Glow to Gold

But out of the corner of his EYE,
                      Something appears to him close BY.

          He immediately looks over
        To what grabbed his ATTENTION.

         It is a purple glow in the hay,
           Then Tazan says…

TAZAN: Hummm, I see something you forgot to
       MENTION. I wonder what it could be.

   Tazan begins to slither over to the GLOW.
Shine runs ahead as fast as she can,
              Dives in front of him, and says…

SHINE: **NO**! You're going to have to get through me first!

TAZAN: If you knew what was best for you, you'd back away, girl.

         Shine picks up rocks
       And throws them at TAZAN.

      She's trying her best to stop him
From finding what's underneath that WAGON.

      TAZAN: Ahhurrrr, I warned you!

          Tazan gets mad
      And thrusts his hand FORWARD.

Meant to grab Shine,
       But Blinding jumps in to save her,
             Landing in his hand of TORTURE.

         SHINE: Blinding!

Tazan: Hahaha, well, isn't this perfect! A little
   Golden boy trying to save the girl.

Blinding: You are weak and a coward, Tazan! You would
   really destroy a defenseless Golden One just to get
   what you want? Is that who you are, tough guy?

   Tazan pulls Blinding to his face,
   Looking him right in the EYE.

   And for what seems like the first time ever,
   Tazan says the truth and not a deceitful LIE.

Tazan: You must not know me very well, boy. I would
   destroy everything just to get what I want.

   Then Tazan's eyes glow blood red,
   Making Blinding's eyes glow the SAME.

   And out of Blinding's mouth,
   The light from his heart CAME.

Tazan, with his eyes,
   Sucks out all of Blinding's light.
Tazan then tosses his lightless body to the GROUND.
   Looking over at Shine,
He just smiles and doesn't make a SOUND.

Back over to the witches,
Aldin and the two creatures of GREEN.
   Their fighting still continues,
               Endlessly it SEEMS.

Witches: We will never give up! The storm must go on!

   The two green creatures make a force FIELD,

Glow to Gold

Wrapping up the two witches.
They bind them to the ground in a SHIELD.

Then Aldin grabs one of the other two witches,
Pulling her CLOSE.

He puts her hand on his chest,
Over his Golden-flamed heart.
Her hand slowly turns to GOLD,

And the look on her face
Shows that she KNOWS.

The other two witches break free from their force field,
And Aldin lets the witch he has GO.

Knowing the love of Aziz is real,
The two green creatures slowly back away,
With their faces showing so FRIGHTENEDLY.

And the four witches all form together as one,
Growing big and tall and MIGHTY.

Witches: We will never surrender!

The one great witch
Then chases after the two green CREATURES.

And Tazan, talking to Shine,
Tries to deceive her,
As if he's an all-knowing PREACHER.

Tazan: You know, Shine, you chose to see me as a monster. I don't blame you. You were born, raised, and taught to believe that I am. But if I am truly the monster Aziz claims me to be, then why would the Almighty Aziz allow the Golden Ones that he loves so dearly to go through so much destruction and pain? It's torture, I presume. How could an Almighty, all-knowing, all-powerful, and loving Aziz allow this to happen? Because it's all a lie! The greatest lie ever told. Look at all you Golden Ones: begging, hoping, keeping your faith, but for what? You're all miserable, failing, and about to become slaves! You Golden Ones have a choice though, Shine. You all can choose to keep believing in this treacherous lie, or you all could choose to accept the truth: that Aziz is a lie. Give up on that useless faith, hope, and love, and join me and my army. Live free, with power! Know what it's like to be almighty and never have to follow a rule or a command. The choice is always yours. I'll give you a moment to pray about it. Ha-ha-ha. See if your Aziz really comes through.

Shine falls to her KNEES.
She closes her eyes,
Bows her head,
And starts moving her lips, talking to AZIZ.

Back to the fight on the other SIDE,
The two green creatures are running from the one great witch.
They crawl under big rocks to HIDE.

Aldin shouts out to the one great witch,
But she seems not to HEAR.

Aldin shouts out again,
And the words he says
Send fearful truth down their EARS.

ALDIN: You know, y'all are just like the Golden Ones! There's light inside you! All you have to do is let it shine!

The one great witch just IGNORED.
Instead of having love,
They would rather have the SWORD.

Glow to Gold

ALDIN: You know you're just like the Golden Ones! There's light inside you! All you have to do is let it shine!

The one great witch, filled with anger,
Turns her HEAD.

Looking straight at Aldin, she screams and says…

ONE GREAT WITCH: Ahh, the light is a lie! Love is DEAD!

Aldin, knowing he's about to have to do something
That he really doesn't WANT,

Knows it is something that must be done,
For the one great witch will stop at nothing
Until her destruction FLOUNTS.

The one great witch rushes towards ALDIN.

Aldin turns his head,
Closes his eyes,
And sticks his hand out, GROWLING.

ALDIN: Uhhrrrrr!

When she gets an inch close,
Aldin shoots a blast of light from his HAND.

He blinds the one great witch,
And she falls down to the LAND.

ALDIN: Accept the light or burn away in despair.

ONE GREAT WITCH: Do what you must, but it's the storm you should beware. Ahhhhh!

With the one great witch casting down a bolt of LIGHTNING,
Aldin has to do something that goes against love
Just to stop the FIGHTING.

Aldin puts his hand over her heart,
Doing what he MUST.

He blasts her into a great big ball of fire.
She yells…

One Great Witch: No!

And then she burns away to DUST.

Back to Tazan,
Shine stands up to SPEAK.

The faith she has in Aziz
Is extraordinary and UNIQUE.

TAZAN: Hahahaha, Aziz the great and powerful
is going to show himself? Ha-ha-ha-ha!

SHINE: Tazan, you're wrong! Aziz is coming,
right now! One, two, three!

As soon as she says three,
Beyond the storm, a beam of light shoots THROUGH,

Landing directly on a Glowie.
The light turns him into a frozen Golden STATUE.

Blink, blink

A sound greater than thunder strikes,
Rumbling through the LAND.

Glow to Gold

Tazan's body shakes from such great fear
As he trembles to the ground like SAND.

Shine: Who's the one that's lying now, huh?

Tazan knows the storm is about to go AWAY.
He swipes Shine into his hand
And then proceeds to say…

Tazan: No! I will have it my WAY!

Tazan slithers as fast as he can
Back into the Gloomy NIGHT.

Still set on doing his evil will,
He takes with him all he can of LIGHT.

Tazan: We have to go back, my Glowies! Gather the Golden men in the cages of lightning! And everything you see with light, take it and bring it back with you! Let's go, Glowies, hurry!

The Glowies take up the Golden men,
And then they all rush back HOME.

Out of the hole come running Greeby and Sfary,
Not knowing anything that's gone ON.

Greeby: Whuuu, sorry that took a minute. What did we miss?

The Glowie army comes running through
with Tazan to RETREAT.
Greeby and Sfary jump into each other and begin to SCREAM.

Greeby and Sfary: Ahh, ahhhh!

ALDIN: No!

Pulling behind a cage of lightning,
Greeby and Sfary get thrown IN.

Managing to pop her arm out of Tazan's clutches,
Shine shouts out…

SHINE: Aldin!

ALDIN: Shine!

One of the green creatures finally crawls out
From under the rocks,
But he gets picked up as WELL.

The other green creature shows a face of pain and sadness
As he reaches his hands out with a silent YELL.

The Glowies are gone, and the storm has passed AWAY.
The light from the sun will shine forever,
And the Golden Day will always STAY.

All that remains are the women and CHILDREN,
The green creature and Aldin,
And Spark and Q-PIT.
They all gather to the Castle of GOLD,
Looking devastatingly shaken,
No one talking or saying a WORD.

Spark points to the lightless body of BLINDING.
Q-Pit then runs up to Aldin, and he swears he hears him say…

Q-PIT: Follow me and pick up his body. There's
a gift up ahead worth FINDING.

Aldin walks and picks up the body of BLINDING.
He takes a few steps forward and sees an open gate inside a hole
With a riddle to the gift that's HIDING.

Aldin reads the same riddle
That everyone else can READ.

But underneath, glowing in purple,
Is another note that only he can SEE.

ALDIN: What is this?

There is no light too great,
Just as there is no light too small,
But the only way to enter inside is to have no light at all.
Hiding in the darkness ahead lies life's greatest secret,
And only the one who was given the Eyes of Truth
Wields the power to reveal it.

If you're able to read this last step, then you must be the one.
Take a hold of what was found, let it into your
heart, and you will harness the sun.
This is only possible to achieve by having true love's feel, and
the mighty strength in your belief is what makes it all real.

Aldin, still holding Blinding's body,
Walks down into the ROOM.

Turning from Golden to Glow,
Aldin feels like this room is a TOMB.

Aldin sees nothing inside and places Blinding DOWN.

He then turns off his Glow, and something
unexpected is FOUND.

HOLY: Ah, ha, finally you show up. I've been waiting down here for centuries. Good to meet you, young man. I am the departed ghost, but you can call me Holy. And you are?

ALDIN: Well, umm, I'm Aldin. I know I shouldn't be questioning anything anymore, but you're real, right? This is really happening? I've never seen a ghost before. What is that?

HOLY: Yes, this is real, and I'm much more than just a ghost. I am part of Aziz. I bring gifts to all the Golden Ones who accept me into their hearts. Dipping themselves in the Pond of Bluest Water to wash away their old selves is the only way to allow me in to gift you and clean you up. Once I am accepted inside their hearts, Aziz will always be with them.

ALDIN: So why are you in here? Why are you not out there telling them this? Tazan has destroyed their faith and stolen pretty much every Golden One out there. Look what he has done to Blinding. The people are scared. They never knew their light could be gone or go out forever. There are only women and children left. How are they supposed to fight off Tazan and his army? We're just going to lose. All hope is lost. I tried to help, but I feel I'm the one that made this all happen.

HOLY: I'm not hiding, Aldin. I was forgotten, and you seeing me means not all hope is lost. Anything is possible with Aziz. You see this door here with a lock?

ALDIN: Whoa, where did that come from? How did you…

HOLY: Never mind that. Now that you
see the door, pass through it.

Aldin twists and turns the handle,
                              But nothing.

It won't OPEN.

He pulls the chain and pulls the lock,
        Rams the door,
                But nothing is BROKEN.

ALDIN: I can't pass through. It's locked up. I'd need a key to open it.

HOLY: No, that's where you're wrong, Aldin. Aziz can open any door no matter how locked up it may seem. Just as you and the few people left can defeat Tazan and free the Golden Ones.

ALDIN: Okay, and how?

HOLY: Accepting me into your heart will allow Aziz to work all wonders and possibilities. The fact that you, Aldin, can see me means you are the one to remind the people of that. Have them accept me, and I assure you, Aziz will be with all of you and you will win. Anything is possible with Aziz, and no door can't be walked through with Aziz. Accept me into your heart, Aldin, and Aziz will walk you through this door. Beyond this door is the faith, hope, and love that needs to be restored. Do you accept me, Aldin?

ALDIN: I accept you, Holy Ghost, to come into my heart and wash away the old me.

HOLY: You have freed me, Aldin. Have all the others accept me in the Pond of Bluest Water. Here is your gift.

Holy closes his eyes,
        Spreads his arms out,
                And flows inside Aldin's HEART.

Aldin is filled with the Holy Ghost,

Feeling brand new and that this is a new START.

Aldin looks at the door,
Still CONFUSED.

He goes to grab the knob,
But his hand goes THROUGH.

Aldin: That's weird. Can I just…

Aldin puts his arm through the door,
Then he walks straight THROUGH.
Then he hears this voice in his head saying…

Holy: I told you no doors are locked and anything is possible with Aziz. The impossible only comes from YOU.

A pure white altar is standing there;
Aldin sees it right in FRONT.
On top of the altar is a white stone HEART.

Feeling that it has been chipped,
He begins to read the NAME.

The name that Aldin speaks out loud is…

Aldin: The Sun of FLAMES…

Aldin then wipes off the dust and blows it away.
He sees a different name now written WITHIN.

The name that he reads out loud now is his name…

Aldin: ALDIN…

He then takes the white stone heart and
puts it into his own HEART.

Aldin bursts into flames of gold,
With flaming eyes of blue.
His heart is now a flame of gold,
And his light casts out the DARK.
Aldin's light now shines bright,
Turning everything glittery and GOLD.

Then he passes through the door.
Looking down, he sees a lightless body of OLD.

Aldin picks up the lightless body of Blinding
And emerges into the Golden DAY.

Looking so bright and shiny,
Everyone notices, gasping with amazement and awe.
They point and SAY…

GOLDEN WOMEN AND CHILDREN: Look! It's the Sun of **FLAMES**!

Aldin drops down on a knee
And lays on the ground the lightless body of BLINDING.

Aldin then puts his hand on his chest,
Breathing in light through his mouth.
His heart suddenly starts glowing and SHINING.

Blinding's eyes begin to open, and he
is resurrected back to LIFE.
His body shines tenfold with light and gold,
And he asks…

BLINDING: What happened? Who are you? Am I **ALIVE**?

Aldin just smiles.
Then he stands,
Offering out to Blinding a helping HAND.

Blinding grabs hold,
And up he stands.
Looking out and around, he sees
A distorted and wasted LAND.

All the people left
Crowd around the one they believe is the Sun of FLAMES.

Then all fall to their knees and begin to worship,
Thanking him and praising his NAME.

ALDIN: No, stand up, please, stand up. Do not worship me. I am no greater than any of you. I am one with you, and we are one body together. Follow me to the Pond of Bluest Water. I will dip you inside. The water will wash you clean, and if you accept the spirit of Holy into your hearts, Aziz will be with you, and you will receive a gift from Holy. That gift is unique and special for each individual. It will allow us as one to defeat Tazan, save our Golden families, and let the light of the Golden Day outshine all darkness. Come, it's time to make ourselves brand new!

All the people follow Aldin to the Pond of Bluest WATER.
The creature of green,
Blinding,
And Aldin work together,
Dipping them in to wash away the pain from being a MARTYR.

ALDIN: Do you accept the spirit of Holy into your heart?

GOLDEN WOMEN: I do.

One by one, they are dipped in the water and washed CLEAN,

Glow to Gold

Each one receiving a gift.
The belief that Aziz is with them is now surely SEEN.

While this is taking place here,
There is still horror to be found deep
inside the Gloomy NIGHT.

Tazan is still turning Golden Ones to Glowies,
Stealing their light,
And filling himself up with such anger,
Hatred,
And SPITE.

TAZAN: There is no way I can lose now. Not with all your lights! And when I'm done taking all of yours, I will then take Shine's. Ha-ha! WyUlle, I've changed my mind; this light will be yours to take.

Tazan slithers over to Shine with a creepily evil SMILE.
While back in the Golden Day,
Aldin and the people are marching forward in line,
Single FILE.

ALDIN: Remember everyone! Aziz is with us! The weakness of a Glowie is that they have light inside them! The only way to defeat them is by letting that light shine! When we get to the Gloomy Night, you all stand behind me. Side by side, stretching across the Gloomy Night from the Great Tree all the way to the beginning of the Dark Forest! This little creature of green will enter before we do. He will lead the way and then call us forward. When we are called, we will march across the Gloomy Night, casting out all darkness!

Aldin looks down at the green creature.
He smiles and says…

ALDIN: Do you like your new gift? You look very happy and seem filled with great EXCITEMENT.

The green creature smiles,
Dances,
Moves his arms,
And magic begins to play.
Every Golden One in the line
He is able to use as an INSTRUMENT.

In the Gloomy Night,
Tazan is done turning all the Golden Ones into GLOWIES.

Shine is the only one left with light,
But WyUlle wants to lock her away like a TROPHY.

WYULLE: Let's keep her like this, Father. Let her watch her kingdom fall and let her be our reminder of all our great accomplishments.

TAZAN: I like how you think, WyUlle, but this light inside her is the light that you need to become as I am. Only her light can bring you that. So go ahead, take it. Take her light!

Shine is chained down center stage,
Unable to talk or MOVE.

All the Glowies are circled around, watching
And waiting to see how her light transforms WYULLE.

WyUlle stares deep at Shine, and his eyes
glow blood red like TAZAN's.
Then the sound of music plays,
And Tazan hears an old familiar sound of what
was once called the Golden BAND.

Glow to Gold

Tazan quickly turns his head,
        Only seeing the creature of green.
                It begins to make him QUIVER.

      Music plays throughout the land,
And the whole Glowie army starts to SHIVER.

   WyUlle: How is he doing that, Father?

   Tazan: No, this can't be! Only the Sun of
   Flames makes the Golden Band play…

WyUlle: Father, are you saying that his second
coming is true? You told me that was all a lie.

Tazan: And it is a lie, boy! I made sure a long time
ago he would never return! Now rise up, my Glowie
army, go! Take out this ridiculous impostor, attack!

        The other green creature,
        The one that was CAPTURED—

Tazan and his army seem to have forgotten all about him.
          From his cage to the clouds,
                The creature of green is RAPTURED.

    The Glowie army runs up, and the green
        creature holds out his finger,
    Gesturing for them all to stay STILL.

The Glowie army watches as he dances,
    Moving his arms around, playing music in the air.
  Then a band of Golden Ones starts marching over the HILL.

      The green creature gets carried away,
      Orchestrating the Golden BAND.

With every move the green creature makes,
              He has the Golden Ones forming around, casting out the dark from the LAND.

From a musical tune on the left
To a musical tune on the RIGHT,

The green creature has the Golden Ones dance and play
As he moves them forward through their Gloomy NIGHT.

Aldin walks up with glittering flames of gold,
              His heart a Golden Flame,
                          And his eyes a flame of BLUE.
      The Glowies get scorched from his light,
        And they don't know what to DO.

ALDIN: Stop this war and surrender! Accept the light inside you, and you will be saved! Love awaits you, and it's for every one of you! Come forth, love has not turned you down! If you stay and fight against love, you will be thrown into fire! Please accept the light, and all will be forgiven!

A Glowie then rushes towards Aldin,
Angrily and FUSED.

As soon as the Glowie goes to strike,
Aldin places his hand on his chest,
Bursts him into a ball of fire,
And the Glowie burns away to DUST.

After that, three more Glowies attack,
Thinking for sure Aldin will be CRUSHED.

Aldin bursts them all into fire,
And each one burns away to a pile of DUST.

Glow to Gold

ALDIN: Surrender. Don't fight! Let us ignite that
light inside of you! The love of Aziz will turn
your heart, and you too may shine bright!

All the Glowies tremble to their knees,
        Bowing their heads
                And closing their EYES.

Shaking and scared from what they have done,
They beg for forgiveness and fearfully CRY.

The creature of green starts dancing and playing,
Making music of a happy TUNE.

All the Golden Ones and Aldin
Touch the Glowies on the head, turning them Golden
And marching forward with a bigger band
to cast out all darkness SOON.

Glowing to gold, the truth unfolds,
And Tazan slithers away to HIDE.

Grabbing Shine and taking her with him,
WyUlle yells out…

WYULLE: You **LIED**! You lied about everything!

Tazan puts his fingers over his lips,
And in a panic, he gestures to be SILENT.

WyUlle screams, then speaks out…

WYULLE: Ahhhh, no! Now is not the time to be **QUIET**!

Music plays, and Aldin,
        The green creature,

And all the Golden Ones surround THEM.

The light has covered almost everything,
Leaving the Gloomy Night very SLIM.

The only darkness left in their world
Is the exile where Tazan and WyUlle SIT.

Everything else is now under the light of the Golden Day's sun,
And soon the rest of the Gloomy Night
will become one with IT.

Aldin shows his face to his brother
And then offers out his HAND.

WyUlle, enraged, says to Aldin…

WyUlle: Ha-ha-ha, you are not the Sun of Flames. Father never lied, he was right, and you should have never come back to our **LAND**!

WyUlle strikes,
    But the other green creature flies from the clouds
        And binds WyUlle to the ground in CHAINS.

Then the green creature takes WyUlle,
    Wrapping him up in a force field
And dragging him into exile where he shall forever REMAIN.

All the Golden Ones,
The green creature, and Aldin
Begin to surround Tazan,
Making it so that he can't ESCAPE.

Tazan then grins the biggest smile
And takes a very frightening SHAPE.

Glow to Gold

TAZAN: You will pay greatly for your mistakes.

Tazan spins in a circle,
Squeezing Shine tightly wrapped within his TAIL.

He smiles a gruesome smile before swallowing Shine whole.
Then suddenly, he's turned back into a SNAIL.

TAZAN: What? How did…

SUN OF FLAMES: Tazan!

Tazan turns to see the glory of the true Sun of FLAMES.
Everyone around is in awe of his beauty,
While Tazan trembles with fear.
Then the Sun of Flames says…

SUN OF FLAMES: You should be ASHAMED.

He releases Shine from her chains,
And she runs to Aldin HUGGING.
Everybody except Tazan is feeling the most out of LOVING.

TAZAN: Please, Aziz, have mercy on me. I never hurt anyone. You can give me another chance, right? I deserve it, please!

SUN OF FLAMES: Tazan, I've let you roam free and never interfered with you. You took it upon yourself to hurt and destroy these good people. The only second chance I'll give you is to live out in exile for eternity. Do you accept?

TAZAN: Oh yes, thank you, oh great one. I really admire your—

SUN OF FLAMES: Go, Tazan! You are never to return to the Golden Day.

Tazan runs into exile.
Quickly, he DISAPPEARS.

All the Golden Ones dance with joy
As they clap their hands and CHEER.

ALDIN: I told you I met your father.

Shine looks up with tears falling from her EYES.
Her father walks up, wiping them away, and says…

SUN OF FLAMES: Hi there, my dear Shine.
There is no need to CRY.

SHINE: Ah, I've missed you so much.

SUN OF FLAMES: I have too, daughter. I know I was gone, but I was always still with you.

Shine and her father hug each other TIGHT.
Then Q-Pit comes running up,
Smiling with such DELIGHT.

Everyone is smiling and happy,
For that evil lives no MORE.
Aldin then takes the stage,
Shining like never BEFORE.

ALDIN: Okay everyone! Let's go to the Pond of Bluest Water to wash our old selves clean! Let the spirit of Holy into your heart, and amazing gifts he will bring!

Now all are at the pond,
Washing clean and receiving GIFTS.

Aldin is walking to the Sun of Flames,

Glow to Gold

Then quickly he SHIFTS.

Aziz: Aldin, please come speak with me.

Aldin: Yes, sir?

Aziz: Haha, I want to thank you, Aldin. You have been very brave and very courageous. I know you would be a perfect fit for my Shine. You can just call me Pops from now on, son-in-law. Ha-ha-ha. Now give me a hug!

They hug, and Shine is SMILING.
Greeby and Sfary are in the back, showing off and STYLING.

Greeby: Hey, Sfary, check this out. Boom! I just turned this stone gold. Ha-ha. What's your gift?

Sfary touches the ground, and a rose blooms out,
Smiling from the SIGHT.

He picks it up without a word,
Then brings it to his girl, LIGHT.

Greeby: Well, that's a cool gift, I guess.

Greeby scratches his HEAD.
Then Bright walks by.
Quickly, he turns his head, quickly chasing after her he goes,
But he trips INSTEAD.

Greeby: Hey, my little Bright Golden Gir. Ahhhh!

Blinding and the girl he locked eyes with finally get to MEET.
They find a bench close by and both take a SEAT.

Shine and Aldin are both talking and laughing.

She says…

SHINE: This is the best day EVER!

And before Aldin can say a word,
Everything and everyone seem to freeze TOGETHER.

ALDIN: Shine? Hello? What is going on?
Why is everyone frozen still?

Aldin begins to walk around, feeling very strange and WEIRD.
Then he starts to think the worst:
that Tazan is back, he FEARED.

Afraid and SHOCKED,

He stays PUT,
Not knowing where to GO.

Entering in from another dimension
Is a red-colored cartoon figure
Whose name is

MILO.

MILO: Hi, I'm Milo, the Red Dragon!
Are you ready to go on a fun learning adventure with me?

Alright! Well, follow me.

Glow to Gold

GLOW 2 GOLD

The Diamond Army

Late one night, when the blood-red moon has reached its **PEAK**,
In the darkest part of exile, Tazan awakes from his **SLEEP**.
Shivering from the cold and with nowhere to **GO**,
he slams his fist to the ground, breaking open a **HOLE**.
Too dark to see but hearing crumbling **UNDERNEATH**,
Tazan falls through the cracks, landing into a jaw of red **TEETH**.
The light from the moon made the teeth **GLOW**,
revealing a long-lost cave of ancient and **OLD**.
Tazan slowly rises up, baffled by what he's **FOUND**.
Standing in a sea of diamonds, this was the ruins of a **BATTLEGROUND**.
Long before Aziz created the golden **ONES**,
there were many unfathomable creatures that needed to be **SHUNNED**.
Bound from existence, Tazan stares at the creature's **REMAINS**.
An evil grin grew upon his face, and Tazan says,

"This is my new army. I will **REIGN**."